1992

ZAGAT BOSTON RESTAURANT SURVEY

**Edited by Corby Kummer
and
Jane Heald Lavine**

Published and Distributed by

ZAGAT SURVEY
4 Columbus Circle
New York, New York 10019
212-977-6000

To Julia Child,
Who Inspires Us All

©1991 Eugene H. Zagat, Jr. and Nina S. Zagat
ISBN 0-943421-45-4

ACKNOWLEDGMENTS

We gratefully acknowledge the assistance of the following people: David Archer, Sarah Ehrlich, Jerry Finegold, Harvey Finkel, Michele Fishel, K. Dun Gifford, Stephen Huber, Nancy Jenkins, Chas Lavine, Mirtha Mateo, Louise Natenshon, Frank Primavera, Wendy Ruggiero, Gail Sacramoni, Heidi Schuster, Julie Waters, Barry Weisman and Lauren Weisman.

FOR INFORMATION ON ORDERING

ZAGAT UNITED STATES TRAVEL SURVEY
3 volumes covering over 1500 hotels, resorts, spas, airlines and car rental companies

or

ZAGAT RESTAURANT SURVEYS
Arizona; Atlanta; Baltimore; Boston; Chicago; Dallas–Fort Worth; Hawaii; Houston; Kansas City; Los Angeles–Southern California; Miami–Southern Florida; Montreal; New Orleans; New York City; Suburban New York City; Orlando–Central Florida; Pacific Northwest; Philadelphia; St. Louis; San Francisco and Washington, D.C.

or

ZAGAT NYC MARKETPLACE SURVEY
covering food, wine and entertaining sources

Call 212-977-6000
or write to:

Zagat Survey
4 Columbus Circle
New York, New York 10019

Regarding Corporate Gifts and Deluxe Editions, call 212-977-6000

CONTENTS

Introduction	7
Foreword	8
Explanation of Ratings and Symbols	9
Boston's Most Popular Restaurants	10
Top Ratings	
• Top Food and by Cuisine	11
• Top Decor, Views, Rooms, Service	14
Best Buys	16
ALPHABETICAL DIRECTORY,	
RATINGS AND REVIEWS	
• Boston	19
• Cape Cod, Martha's Vineyard and Nantucket	98
• Rhode Island	102
• New Hampshire and Maine	105
INDEXES	
• Types of Cuisine	108
• Neighborhood Locations	117
• Bar Scenes	126
• Breakfast	126
• Business Dining	127
• BYO Wine or Beer	127
• Caters	128
• Dancing	128
• Delivers	128
• Dessert and Ice Cream	129
• Dining Alone	130
• Entertainment	130
• Fireplaces	131
• Game in Season	131
• Garden/Outdoor Dining	133
• Happy Hour	133
• Health/Spa Menus	134
• Historic Interest	134
• Hotel Dining	135
• "In" Places	136
• Jacket/Tie Required	136
• Late Dining	137
• Noteworthy Newcomers	137
• Offbeat	137
• Parking/Valet	138
• Parties	139
• Private Rooms	142
• People-Watching	144

- Power Scenes 144
- Pre-Theater/Early-Bird Menus 144
- Post-Theater/Prix-Fixe Menus 145
- Reservations Essential 145
- Reservations Not Accepted 146
- Romantic Spots 147
- Saturday Dining 147
- Senior Appeal 151
- Sidewalk Cafes 152
- Sleepers 152
- Smoking Prohibited 152
- Sunday Dining 153
- Takeout 157
- Teas 159
- Teenagers & Other Youthful Spirits ... 159
- Visitors on Expense Accounts 160
- Wheelchair Access 160
- Winning Wine Lists 163
- Worth a Trip 164
- Young Children 164

Rating Sheets 167
Wine Chart 171

INTRODUCTION

Here are the results of our new *Boston Restaurant Survey*, covering over 500 restaurants in the Boston area, including some outstanding places on Cape Cod, Martha's Vineyard and Nantucket, and as far away as Rhode Island, New Hampshire and Maine. Some 1,300 people participated in this *Survey*. Since the participants dined out an average of 2.8 times per week, this *Survey* is based on roughly 190,000 meals eaten in area restaurants annually.

Knowing that the quality of this *Survey* is the direct result of their thoughtful voting and commentary, we sincerely thank each participant. They include numerous professionals, business executives and just plain folks – food lovers all.

By surveying large numbers of local restaurant-goers, we think we have achieved a uniquely current and reliable guide. We hope you agree. On the assumption that most people want a "quick fix" on the places at which they are considering eating, we have tried both to be concise and to provide handy indexes.

We are especially grateful to our editors, Corby Kummer, writer and editor with *The Atlantic* magazine, and Jane Heald Lavine, a food consultant and a partner in a Boston-based event planning concern.

We invite you to be a reviewer in our next Survey. To do so, simply send a stamped, self-addressed, business-size envelope to ZAGAT SURVEY, 4 Columbus Circle, New York, N.Y. 10019 so that we will be able to contact you. Each participant will receive a free copy of the next *Boston Restaurant Survey* when it is published.

Your comments, suggestions and criticisms of this *Survey* are also solicited. There is always room for improvement – with your help.

New York, New York Nina and Tim Zagat
September 1, 1991

FOREWORD

The demise of the Massachusetts Miracle has brought a miracle for Boston diners: a return to good value at restaurants everywhere in New England. The most telling change between this Boston *Survey* and our last *Survey* is one you can't see. The average estimated price of a meal with one drink and tip has actually dropped at most restaurants that appeared in our last *Survey*. The success of lower-priced cafes and menu items showed the way for owners of restaurants, who have bowed to the new reality that people watch much more carefully where their restaurant dollar goes.

The result is a wider choice of excellent restaurants of all kinds for less money. Bostonians are a pretty trend-resistant lot – they're more interested in good food. Their loyalty has kept local restaurants at a level of expertise and originality that only a handful of other cities can match. Chefs such as Jasper White (of Jasper's), Lydia Shire (of Biba), Gordon Hamersley (of Hamersley's Bistro), Frank McClelland (of L'Espalier), Michela Larson (of Michela's), Chris Schlesinger (of East Coast Grill) and Todd English (of Olives) have all been nationally acclaimed for their re-thought New England dishes and bold branching out, too. Outside Boston, the talents of Johanne Kileen and George Germon (of Providence's Al Forno and Lucky's), Robert Raban (of Cape Cod's Chillingsworth) and Jean-Charles Berruet (of Nantucket's Chanticleer) are earning them national reputations as well.

From Downtown to Faneuil Hall, from the Waterfront, Back Bay and Beacon Hill to Cambridge, Brookline and the suburbs, there are wonderful finds all over Boston and restaurants of national caliber in adjacent states, as well as Cape Cod, Martha's Vineyard and Nantucket. You'll find them all in this book.

Boston, MA
September 1, 1991

Corby Kummer
Jane Heald Lavine

EXPLANATION OF RATINGS AND SYMBOLS

FOOD, DECOR and **SERVICE** are each rated on a scale of 0 to 30 in columns marked **F, D** and **S:**

- 0-9 = poor to fair
- 10-19 = good to very good
- 20-25 = very good to excellent
- 26-30 = extraordinary to perfection

The **COST** column, headed by a **C**, reflects the estimated price of a dinner with one drink and tip. As a rule of thumb, lunch will cost 25 percent less.

An **Asterisk (*)** after a restaurant's name means the number of persons who voted on the restaurant is too low to be statistically reliable; **L** for late means the restaurant serves after 11 PM; **S** or **M** means it is open on Sunday or Monday respectively; **X** means no credit cards are accepted.

By way of **Commentary**, we attempt to summarize the comments of the *Survey* participants. The prefix **U** means comments were uniform; **M** means they were mixed.

The names of the restaurants with the highest overall ratings and greatest popularity are printed in solid capital letters, e.g., "**BIBA**."

If we do not show ratings on a restaurant, it is either an important **newcomer** or a popular **write-in**; however, comments are included and the estimated cost, including one drink and tip, is indicated by the following symbols:

- **I** = below $15
- **M** = $15 to $30
- **E** = $30 to $50
- **VE** = $50 or above

BOSTON'S MOST POPULAR RESTAURANTS

Each of our reviewers has been asked to name his or her five favorite restaurants. The 40 spots in the metropolitan Boston area most frequently named, in order of their popularity, are:

1. Biba
2. Legal Sea Foods
3. Olives
4. Hamersley's Bistro
5. Jasper's
6. Aujourd'hui
7. East Coast Grill
8. Michela's
9. Ritz Dining Room
10. L'Espalier
11. Locke-Ober Cafe
12. Seasons
13. Bay Tower Room
14. Skipjack's
15. Davio's
16. Ristorante Toscano
17. Icarus
18. Maison Robert
19. Grill 23
20. Julien
21. Cornucopia
22. Morton's
23. Cafe Budapest
24. Another Season
25. Bertucci's
26. St. Cloud
27. Dali
28. Pillar House
29. Green Street Grill
30. 798 Main
31. Harvard Street Grill
32. Cottonwood Cafe
33. Daily Catch
34. Harvest
35. Jimmy's Harborside
36. Rowes Wharf
37. Redbones
38. Chez Nous
39. Davide
40. Border Cafe

It's obvious that good things come at a price – most of the popular restaurants above are also among the city's most expensive. However, Bostonians love a bargain. Were popularity calibrated to price, we suspect that a number of other restaurants would join the above ranks. Accordingly, we have put together lists of Boston's Top Bangs for the Buck and Good Values on pages 16 and 17.

TOP RATINGS*

TOP 40 FOOD RATINGS
(In order of rating)

27 – Olives
L'Espalier
26 – Hamersley's Bistro
Jasper's
Seasons
Aujourd'hui
Julien
25 – Biba
Chez Nous
798 Main
Harvard Street Grill
24 – Gyuhama
Cornucopia
Ristorante Toscano
Giacomo's
East Coast Grill
Morton's
Icarus
Davide
Five Seasons
Michela's
Takeshima
Upstairs at the Pudding
Le Bocage
Dali
23 – Legal Sea Foods
Green Street Grill
Oasis Cafe
Rarities
Plaza Dining Room
Chau Chow
Mister Leung's
Maison Robert
Davio's
Rita's Place
Carl's Pagoda
Roka
Parker's
Ritz Dining Room
22 – Grill 23

TOP SPOTS BY CUISINE

**Top American
(Contemporary)**
26 – Jasper's
Seasons
25 – 798 Main Street
24 – Cornucopia
Icarus

**Top American
(Traditional)**
23 – Oasis Cafe
Union Grill
Parker's
21 – On the Park
Copley's

Top BBQ
24 – East Coast Grill
21 – Redbones
Jimmy Mac's
20 – Porterhouse Cafe
19 – Bob the Chef

Top Burgers
22 – St. Cloud
21 – Charlie's
20 – Mr. Bartley's
19 – Rocco's
St. Botolph

---

*Excluding restaurants with voting too low to be statistically reliable. Restaurants listed are exclusively in the metropolitan Boston area except where noted.

Top Chinese
- **23** – Chau Chow
  Mister Leung's
  Carl's Pagoda
- **22** – Ho Yuen Ting
- **21** – Mary Chung

Top Chowder
- **23** – Legal Sea Foods
- **21** – Skipjack's
- **20** – Turner Fisheries
  Dover Sea Grille
- **18** – Jimmy's Harborside

Top Continental
- **23** – Parker's
  Ritz Dining Room
- **22** – Cafe Budapest
- **21** – Ritz Cafe
  Locke-Ober Cafe

Top Delis/Sandwiches
- **21** – Charlie's
- **20** – Rebecca's
- **19** – Rubin's
  Great Stuff
- **18** – S&S Restaurant

Top Eclectic
- **27** – Olives
- **26** – Hamersley's Bistro
- **25** – Biba
  Chez Nous
  Harvard St. Grill

Top French Classic
- **23** – Maison Robert
  Ritz Dining Room
- **20** – Veronique
- **19** – Brasserie Les Halles
- **17** – Chez Jean

Top French Nouvelle
- **27** – L'Espalier
- **26** – Aujourd'hui
  Julien
- **25** – Chez Nous
- **24** – Le Bocage

Top Greek/Mid-East
- **22** – Sultan's Kitchen
- **21** – Demo's
- **18** – Karoun
  Sami's 24 Hours
- **17** – Nadia's Eastern Star

Top Hotel Dining
- **26** – Seasons
  Aujourd'hui
  Julien
- **23** – Rarities
  Plaza Dining Room

Top Indian
- **22** – India Pavilion
- **20** – Shalimar of India
- **19** – Taste of India
- **18** – Kebab-n-Kurry
- **17** – Tandoor House

Top Italian
- **24** – Ristorante Toscano
  Giacomo's
  Davide
- **23** – Rita's Place
- **22** – Daily Catch

Top Italian Nuova Cucina
- **24** – Michela's
  Upstairs/Pudding
- **23** – Davio's
- **22** – Mamma Maria
  Stellina's

Top Japanese
- **24** – Gyuhama
  Takeshima
- **23** – Roka
- **22** – Tatsukichi
  Sakura-bana

Top Landmarks
- **23** – Ritz Dining Room
  Plaza Dining Room
- **21** – Locke-Ober Cafe
- **18** – Hampshire House
- **16** – Union Oyster House

Top Mexican/Tex-Mex
- **22** – Mexican Cuisine
- **21** – Sol Azteca
- **20** – Cottonwood Cafe
  Boca Grande
  Casa Romero

Top Newcomers (Rated)
- **23** – Oasis Cafe
- **21** – Buoniconti's
  Jimmy Mac's
- **20** – Porterhouse Cafe
  Veronique

Top Newcomers (Unrated)
- — Azita
- — Blue Wave
- — Caffe Lampara
- — Jae's Cafe
- — Marino's

Top Pizzerias
- **22** – Santarpio's
- **21** – Galeria Umberto
- **20** – Bertucci's
  Bluestone Bistro
  Sorrento's

Top Portuguese/Spanish/Brazilian
- **24** – Dali
- **20** – Neighborhood
- **19** – Casa Portugal
- **18** – Cafe Brazil
  P.A. Seafood

Top Seafood
- **24** – Giacomo's
- **23** – Legal Sea Foods
- **22** – Daily Catch
  Village Fish
- **21** – Skipjack's

Top Steaks
- **24** – Morton's
- **22** – Grill 23
- **21** – Locke-Ober Cafe
- **19** – Dakota's
  Boodle's of Boston

Top Thai
- **22** – Bangkok Cuisine
  Sawasdee
- **21** – Siam Cuisine
  Thai Cuisine
- **20** – Amarin of Thailand

Top Vacation Dining
- **27** – Chillingsworth (Cape)
  Chanticleer (Nantucket)
- **25** – 21 Federal (Nantucket)
  Regatta/Cotuit (Cape)
  L'Etoile (Martha's Vineyd.)

Top Worth a Trip
- **27** – Al Forno (RI)
- **26** – Arrows (ME)
  Lucky's (RI)
- **25** – Angel's (RI)
- **23** – Cape Neddick Inn (ME)

TOP 40 OVERALL DECOR
(In order of rating)

27 – Aujourd'hui
   Ritz Dining Room
26 – Bay Tower Room
   L'Espalier
   Julien
25 – Rowes Wharf
   Plaza Dining Room
   Seasons
   Biba
24 – Parker's
   Bristol Lounge
   Rocco's
   Icarus
   Copley's
   Rarities
23 – Spinnaker Italia
   Loading Zone
   Pillar House
   Ritz Cafe
   Jasper's
   Cafe Budapest
22 – Maison Robert
   Veronique
   Locke-Ober Cafe
   Top of the Hub
   Cornucopia
   Hampshire House
   Mister Leung's
   Warren Tavern
21 – Mill Falls
   Cottonwood Cafe
   Grill 23
   Dali
   Mamma Maria
   Michela's
   St. Cloud
   Dakota's
   Hard Rock Cafe
   Another Season
   Cafe Fleuri

TOP VIEWS
(In alphabetical order)

Anthony's Pier 4
Aujourd'hui
Barrett's
Bay Tower Room
Boston Sail Loft
Cambridge Sail Loft
Chart House
Cherrystones
Davio's (Cambridge)
Jimmy's Harborside
Jonah's
Michael's Waterfront
Mill Falls
Ritz Dining Room
Rowes Wharf
Sally Ling's (Hyatt)
Spinnaker Italia
Top of the Hub
Winerie, The

TOP ROOMS
(In alphabetical order)

- Another Season
- Aujourd'hui
- Bay Tower Room
- Biba
- Cafe Budapest
- Changsho
- Charley's (Newbury St.)
- Colorado Publ. Library
- Copley's
- Cornucopia
- Cottonwood Cafe
- Grill 23
- Hampshire House
- Hungry I
- Michela's
- Icarus
- Jasper's
- Julien
- L'Espalier
- Loading Zone
- Locke-Ober Cafe
- Maison Robert
- Mamma Maria
- Mister Leung's
- Parker's
- Plaza Dining Room
- Rarities
- Ritz Dining Room
- Rocco's
- Rowes Wharf
- St. Cloud
- Seasons
- Sfuzzi
- Veronique

TOP 40 OVERALL SERVICE
(In order of rating)

- **26** – Aujourd'hui
  - Seasons
  - Ritz Dining Room
- **25** – Julien
  - Jasper's
  - L'Espalier
- **24** – Parker's
  - Ritz Cafe
  - Chez Nous
- **23** – Plaza Dining Room
  - Rarities
- **22** – Bristol Lounge
  - Miyako
  - Davide
  - Mamma Maria
  - Mister Leung's
  - Harvard Street Grill
  - Rowes Wharf
  - Maison Robert
  - Giacomo's
  - Le Bocage
  - Cafe Budapest
  - Hamersley's Bistro
  - Icarus
  - 798 Main
  - Pillar House
  - Locke-Ober Cafe
  - Takeshima
- **21** – Ristorante Toscano
  - Another Season
  - Bay Tower Room
  - Upstairs at the Pudding
  - Cafe Fleuri
  - Morton's
  - Veronique
  - Grill 23
  - Michela's
  - Copley's
  - Cornucopia
  - Dali

BEST BUYS

TOP 40 BANGS FOR THE BUCK

This list reflects the best dining values in our *Survey*. It is produced by dividing the cost of a meal into the combined ratings for food, decor and service.

1. Galleria Umberto
2. Charlie's Sandwich Shoppe
3. Boca Grande
4. Sami's 24 Hours
5. Caffe Vittoria
6. New Yorker Diner
7. Mr. Bartley's Burger Cottage
8. Pour House
9. Sultan's Kitchen
10. Bertucci's
11. Neighborhood Restaurant
12. Elsie's
13. Oasis Cafe
14. Coolidge Corner Clubhouse
15. Great Stuff
16. Cafe de Paris
17. Blacksmith House
18. Rudy's Cafe
19. New Bridge Cafe
20. Sevens, The
21. Goemon
22. Santarpio's Pizza
23. B&D Deli
24. Bluestone Bistro
25. Milk Street Cafe
26. Blue Diner
27. S&S Restaurant
28. Cafe Paradiso
29. Bob the Chef
30. Thai House
31. Il Dolce Momento
32. Pentimento
33. Gardner Museum Cafe
34. Thai Cuisine
35. Bel Canto
36. Sorrento's
37. Victoria Diner
38. Siam Cuisine
39. Cornwall's
40. Bangkok Cuisine

ADDITIONAL GOOD VALUES
(A bit more expensive, but worth every penny)

- Acropolis
- Addis Red Sea
- Amarin of Thailand
- Amarin II
- Anchovies
- Bangkok-Tokyo Cafe
- Barbeques International
- Bel Canto
- Bnu
- Border Cafe
- Boston Sail Loft
- Botolph on Tremont
- Bull & Finch Pub
- Buteco
- Cactus Club
- Cafe Brazil
- Cafe China
- Caffe Lampara
- Caffe Luna
- Casa Portugal
- Changsho
- Charley's Saloon
- Chau Chow
- Chef Chang's House
- Chef Chow's House
- Chili's
- Circle Pizza
- Commonwealth Brewing
- Dali
- Demo's
- Division 16
- Dockside
- Downtown Cafe
- Dynasty
- Ethiopian Restaurant
- Fajita Rita's
- Giacomo's
- Golden Palace
- Golden Temple
- Happy Haddock
- Hard Rock Cafe
- Harvard Bookstore Cafe
- Houlihan's
- House of Siam
- Ho Yuen Ting
- Imperial Tea House
- India Pavilion
- Jimbo's Fish Shanty
- Jimmy Mac's
- Johnny D's
- King & I
- Le Grande Cafe
- Little Osaka
- Loading Zone
- Mary Chung
- Massimino's
- Miyako
- Montien
- Nadia's Eastern Star
- New Korea
- Noble House
- Open Sesame
- Pattaya
- Piccolo Venezia
- Pushcart, The
- Redbones
- Roka
- Rubin's
- Sakura-bana
- Sawasdee
- Serendipity III
- Shalimar of India
- Shanghai
- Sol Azteca
- Sports Depot, The
- Star of Siam
- Sunset Cafe
- Sunset Grill & Tap
- Ta Chien
- Takeshima
- Tandoor House
- Taste of India
- TGI Friday's
- Tim's Tavern
- Venetian Gardens
- Venus Seafood
- Weylu's
- Zuma

ALPHABETICAL DIRECTORY OF RESTAURANTS

All Area Codes (617) Unless Otherwise Noted

F	D	S	C

Acapulco/SM | 11 | 10 | 13 | $14 |

266 Newbury St. (bet. Fairfield & Gloucester Sts.), 247-9126
M – Our reviewers say this simple Mexican standby offers "basic, satisfactory food" at low prices and that there's good people-watching on Newbury Street; however, service by "spaced-out" students and "bland" food produce few olés.

Acropolis/SM | 13 | 12 | 15 | $15 |

1680 Massachusetts Ave. (Sacramento St.), Cambridge, 492-0900
M – This Cambridge neighborhood fixture's fans consider it "reliable" for moderately priced Greek-American food; foes figure it's "consistent only in mediocrity" and doesn't live up to its name.

Addis Red Sea | 16 | 15 | 16 | $16 |

544 Tremont St. (bet. Dartmouth & Clarendon Sts.), 426-8727
U – "A slice of Ethiopia" in the South End that has kept a following for its "pleasant atmosphere" and "plentiful", "cheap", "good" food ever since it helped introduce this cuisine to Boston; if sitting on backless stools and eating with your fingers appeals to you, this is a "fun place."

Ahan-Thai and Hong Kong Cuisine | 14 | 16 | 13 | $16 |

(fka Bangkok-Tokyo Cafe)
26 Charles St. (Beacon St.), 723-6570
M – A "nice addition to the neighborhood", this Beacon Hill Asian's elaborate decor gets better reactions than its moderately priced Thai and Chinese menu and its service, which can be "sloppy."

Aku-Aku | 11 | 11 | 13 | $14 |

109 Brookline Ave. (bet. Overland & Burlington Sts.), 536-0420
149 Alewife Pkwy. (intersection of Rtes. 2, 3 & 16), Cambridge, 491-5377
M – "Bad in college, worse now" is one reaction to the "terrible food" and "tacky decor" at these big Chinese-Polynesian eateries, which are in Cambridge and Kenmore Square but "should be in suburban Indianapolis"; on the plus side, the service is "friendly", and if you like sweet "Polynesian" drinks, this is the place.

Boston | F | D | S | C |

Alexander's*/S | 15 | 18 | 18 | $24 |
(fka Villa Anna Ristorante)
1700 Beacon St. (across from Tappan St.), Brookline,
566-3469
*U – After changing names four times in the last two years,
this Continental grill with a Greek accent appears to
have settled into a reliable groove; its tuxedoed service
and somewhat predictable menu might not appeal to
all, but it does what it does well; popular with seniors.*

Amarin of Thailand/SM | 20 | 19 | 18 | $18 |
287 Centre St. (near Galen St.), Newton Corner, 527-5255
*U – This Newton Thai's consistently good food at
moderate prices, "tasteful", "attractive" decor and
"deferential" service all win high marks; possibly a
bit "overrated by suburbanites", it has become a
"family favorite."*

Amarin II | 20 | 17 | 18 | $22 |
27 Grove St. (Spring St.), Wellesley, 239-1350
*U – This Thai "really spices up Wellesley's food scene"
with cooking that, like its Newton Corner sibling, is
"always delicious"; though the room "looks worn", it's
"immaculate", and the eats ensure this place is
continually "crowded" and "outrageously loud."*

Anchovies | – | – | – | I |
433A Columbus Ave. (bet. Braddock & Holyoke Sts.),
266-5088
*A terrific South End neighborhood place, this Southern
Italian newcomer is just the spot to get a hot bowl of
pasta or a first-rate pizza for a reasonable price; it's not
earth-shakingly original, but very good to have around.*

ANOTHER SEASON/M | 22 | 21 | 21 | $34 |
97 Mt. Vernon St. (bet. Charles & W. Cedar Sts.), 367-0880
*U – Chef-owner Odette Bery has kept a loyal clientele
coming to her ground-floor Beacon Hill town-house as
much for her restaurant's "romantic", "intimate" rooms
with whimsical murals and boiseries that recall Paris as
for her "imaginative" French-American food; N.B.
parking is "impossible", and there's no valet.*

Boston | F | D | S | C |

Anthony's Pier 4/SM | 13 | 16 | 14 | $27 |

140 Northern Ave. (on Pier 4), 423-6363
M – To some, an "overrated trap" that "should be closed by the tourist board", this Boston seafood institution nonetheless remains popular, if only as a place to bring out-of-towners; pluses are an excellent wine list (it has won a Grand Award from Wine Spectator magazine), a harborside location and popovers that some remember fondly; minuses are institutional food at cooked-to-order prices, indifferent service and "tired" decor.

Ararat* | 17 | 9 | 17 | $14 |

71 Arlington St. (across from Arsenal Hall), Watertown, 924-4100
U – A "tasty Middle Easterner" with "very reasonable prices", this Watertown ethnic is hardly the city's aesthetic summit, but it's a handy place to grab a bite and "observe yuppiedom."

Atlantic Fish Company/SM | 15 | 15 | 15 | $19 |

777 Boylston St. (near Gloucester St.), 267-4000
M – A formula seafood house with moderate prices, this spot has survived its location near the convention center, is pleasant for sidewalk dining in good weather and has a locally acclaimed pianist at the bar upstairs; otherwise, it's just "middle of the road", best if you "stick to the basics."

AUJOURD'HUI/SM | 26 | 27 | 26 | $48 |

Four Seasons Hotel, 200 Boylston St. (across from Public Garden), 338-4400
U – In just a few years, this "beautiful" room overlooking the Public Garden has established itself as one of Boston's favorites for its "elegant" Nouvelle Continental kitchen – recently taken over by rising-star chef Michael Kornick – and service that makes you feel "pampered"; the Sunday brunch and weekday breakfasts are very popular, and there's an "alternative" low-fat menu, but remember to "bring serious money"; it's not clear yet how the change of chefs will affect the food ratings.

Averof/LSM | 12 | 11 | 14 | $18 |

1924 Massachusetts Ave. (near Porter Sq.), Cambridge, 354-4500
M – Few go for the food, decor or the service at this Porter Square Greek and Middle Eastern eatery; what keeps 'em coming are the low prices and the belly dancing – many agree it's "worth a trip once a year for a hoot."

Boston | F | D | S | C |

Azita | - | - | - | M |

560 Tremont St. (Clarendon St.), 338-8070
More upscale than most local Italians, this South End storefront is a welcome arrival, due to a pleasant room and a personable chef-owner on the premises who exhibits a skilled hand with a small and modestly priced menu; maybe it's not worth a special trip, but the neighborhood loves it.

Back Bay Bistro/SM | 19 | 16 | 17 | $24 |

565 Boylston St. (bet. Clarendon & Dartmouth Sts.), 536-4477
M – This storefront Nouvelle American right on Copley Square is popular for outside dining in warm weather; however, the food is "uneven", with "adventurous combinations" that can be either "intriguing" or "cutesy-poo" and "disappointing", and service that is slow; a recent redecoration also wins mixed reviews.

B & D Deli/SM | 16 | 9 | 12 | $11 |

1653 Beacon St. (bet. University & Winthrop Rds., Washington Sq.), Brookline, 232-3727
835 Beacon St. (Park Ave. & Kenmore Sq.), 859-0087
M – The original Brookline location is a former winner that hasn't recovered from a change of ownership and a renovation (beige Formica tables) that many think left it no better than "standard"; "loud and cramped" for some is a "good neighborhood place" for others, but "New York it ain't"; the new Beacon Street branch is in the Stitches comedy club.

Bangkok Bistro | 18 | 14 | 16 | $16 |

1952 Beacon St. (Cleveland Circle), Brookline, 739-7270
U – A small Cleveland Circle Thai, this storefront uniformly wins praise for its "surprisingly good creative menu", low prices and simple but clean decor; it's a neighborhood find.

Bangkok Cuisine/SM | 22 | 13 | 18 | $16 |

177A Massachusetts Ave. (near Christian Science Ctr. & Berklee College of Music), 262-5377
U – Boston's Best Thai, convenient to Symphony Hall and Berklee College of Music, keeps patrons coming back to its long, narrow room with "unmemorable" decor for "superior pad Thai" as well as coconut soup, curry dishes and spring rolls; the frustratingly slow pre-concert service is said to have improved.

Boston | F | D | S | C |

Barbeques International/SM | 16 | 7 | 16 | $14 |
129 Brighton Ave. (near Harvard St.), Allston, 782-6669
U – Mostly Indian restaurant that offers a "meat fix" that can range from tandoori chicken to BBQ ribs; it's "odorific" and "smoky", but discomfort and scanty decor don't keep our critics away from the bargains.

Barnacle | 19 | 17 | 17 | $17 |
141 Front St. (Sewall St.), Marblehead, 631-4236
M – Most people like the ramshackle charm of this waterside seafoodery, whose long-time fans "always have and always will love" the scenery, the "great chowder", the bloody marys and the "very basic seafood", especially steamers and lobster; dissenters simply find it "acceptable."

Barrett's on Boston Harbour/SM | 15 | 19 | 17 | $23 |
2 Constitution Plaza (next to USS Constitution), Charlestown, 242-9600
U – Bring the relatives for the view of the Constitution and the Boston skyline, but if you don't get a table with a view, "forget it"; the warhorse American food is "high-class Howard Johnson's" at white-tablecloth prices, although the Sunday brunch is popular; P.S. there's always parking in this part of Charlestown.

BAY TOWER ROOM/M | 18 | 26 | 21 | $39 |
60 State St. (Congress St.), 723-1666
U – It's got the "greatest view in Boston", which you "can't eat", but you can and do pay for; the comfortable atmosphere and pleasant service are pluses, and the dance floor makes this the kind of special occasion place where deals are clinched, including the wedding kind, although the traditional American food might not win universal kudos.

Bel Canto/SM | 16 | 13 | 14 | $13 |
42 Charles St. (near Chestnut St.), 523-5575
Wellesley Center, 92 Central St. (near Weston Rd.), Wellesley, 237-2692
1709 Massachusetts Ave. (Lexington Ctr.), Lexington, 861-6556
10 Main St. (Central & Park Sts.), Andover, 508-470-0049
M – Its "healthy" pizza with a whole-wheat crust and vegetarian toppings was a fresh idea in the '70s, but now this local chain seems tired, producing comments such as "too much dough, too little topping", "amateurish" service and "last resort for college students"; nevertheless, many people seem willing to settle for fare that's "decent Italian, nothing special."

Boston | F | D | S | C |

Bella Napoli/LSM | 19 | 12 | 17 | $25 |
425 Hanover St. (near Charter St.), 720-2811
M – This North End Italian has a small but devoted following among our reviewers, who like its Caesar salad and desserts and the valet parking; fewer, however, are impressed by the "intimate" (some say "cramped") decor or the "anything but friendly" service.

Bello Mondo | 18 | 16 | 18 | $27 |
Marriott Copley Place, 110 Huntington Ave. (Copley Pl.), 236-5800
M – It's hard to make hotel restaurants stand out – the Marriott went through several tries before deciding on this Italian formula; many of our reviewers still find it mostly "standard hotel fare" and "bland", though well priced; a few argue "more people should discover this."

Bennett Street Cafe/SM | 17 | 17 | 17 | $22 |
Charles Hotel, 1 Bennett St. (Eliot St.), Cambridge, 864-1200
M – Another metamorphosed hotel dining room, this bright, California-style indoor-outdoor cafe in Harvard Square with paper tablecloths and crayons has won success serving nouvelle pizzas, salads, seafood and Caribbean-style dishes; it's "fun" and a "nice stop for a light meal", despite "shaky" service.

Bennigan's | 13 | 15 | 13 | $16 |
191 Stuart St. (bet. Charles & S. Tremont Sts.), 227-3754
U – Reviled for its plain-chain pub-style food, this is really a singles bar with "very loud music"; however, the Theater District location and late hours are convenient; prepare yourself for "nonexistent service."

Bernardo's | 18 | 12 | 18 | $23 |
24 Fleet St. (bet. Charter & Richmond Sts.), 723-4554
U – Most respondents regard this North End "touch of Italy" as "good but not great", with a "pleasant", unbustling manner that's not quite enough to compensate for the less-than-auspicious decor.

Bernard's | 19 | 12 | 18 | $19 |
Mall at Chestnut Hill, Rte. 9 (bet. Hammond Pond Pkwy. & Langley Rd.), Newton, 969-3388
U – The majority find this "Gucci Chinese" "not bad at all", with many "beautifully served", "unusual combinations"; they only wish the ambiance wasn't "so terribly cold"; on the other hand, most surveyors welcome anything that tastes good at the Mall at Chestnut Hill.

Boston

| F | D | S | C |

BERTUCCI'S BRICK OVEN PIZZERIA/SM | 19 | 15 | 15 | $13 |

17 Commerce Ave. (New Boston St.), 933-1440
39-45 Stanhope St. (bet. Columbus Ave. & Stuart St.), 247-6161
22 Merchants Row (near State St., next to Faneuil Hall), 227-7889
197 Elm St. (Davis Sq.), Somerville, 776-9241
4 Brookline Place (off Boylston St., Rte. 9), Brookline, 731-2300
1 Alewifebrook Pkwy. (near Alewife MBTA station), Cambridge, 876-2200
21 Brattle St. (bet. Church & JFK Sts.), Cambridge, 864-4748
380 Washington St. (bet. Forest St. & Rte. 16), Wellesley, 239-0990
90 Derby St. (near Gardner St.), Hingham, 740-4405
275 Centre St. (Newton Corner), Newton, 244-4900
412 Franklin St. (Five Corners), Braintree, 849-3066
414 Washington St. (at Rtes. 16 & 126), Holliston, 508-429-4571
368 Boston Post Rd. (at Wilson St. & Farm Rd.), 508-460-0911
150 Worcester Rd. (near intersection of Rtes. 9 & 126), Framingham, 508-879-9161
Westgate Mall Plaza, 245 Westgate Rd. (near Rte. 24), Brockton, 508-584-3080
15 Newbury St. (near Rte. 128), West Peabody, 508-535-0969

M – These friendly, noisy places have become family standbys, and the thin-crusted pizza a local standard; most often mentioned in the unusually large number of responses are the crusty dinner rolls, made from pizza dough in brick ovens; the most frequent complaint is inconsistency from one visit and location to the next.

BIBA/LS | 25 | 25 | 17 | $41 |

272 Boylston St..(bet. Arlington St. & Haddassah Way), 426-7878

M – This eclectic newcomer, overlooking the Public Garden, shot straight to the top of Boston's Most Popular List owing to the bold originality of chef-owner Lydia Shire and the "dynamite decor" of designer Adam Tihany; a "must for foodies" since it opened, comments are nonetheless mixed – the "wild food" that draws on India, Asia and many other places is "beautifully prepared and intriguing" to most, but a "puzzle" to some; praise of the always-hopping bar downstairs, with its "great hors d'oeuvre", is mixed with complaints of "spotty" service and noise.

Boston | F | D | S | C |

Bishop's | 21 | 15 | 18 | $22 |
99 Hampshire St. (Lowell St.), Lawrence, 508-683-7143
U – Despite a few complaints that it has "fallen from grace", the majority view is that this old-timer's "great Greek specialties" (especially the "lamb chops you'd kill for") continue to shine, though not the "mega-polyester ambiance."

Bisuteki Japanese Steak House/SM | 17 | 16 | 19 | $21 |
Howard Johnson's Hotel, 777 Memorial Dr. (bet. Harvard & B.U. Bridges), Cambridge, 492-7777
407 Squire Rd., Revere, 284-7200
U – The tableside Samurai knife show at this Japanese-style steak house in the basement of the Cambridge Howard Johnson's has been a known quantity since the '60s; so what if it's "passe" and "all the courses taste the same"? – it's a "fun place" "for a party."

Black Forest Cafe | 18 | 12 | 14 | $17 |
1759 Massachusetts Ave. (Forest & Linnean Sts.), Cambridge, 661-6706
U – This takeout cafe and modest restaurant near Porter Square serving "stir-fry" food is "the way Cambridge was 20 years ago", which means it has simple, none-too-comfortable decor, "ditsy" help and an emphasis on whole-grain foods; exceptions to the good-for-you fare are the "beautiful pastries."

Black Goose | 19 | 17 | 17 | $21 |
(fka Oca Nera)
21 Beacon St. (Bowdoin St.), 720-4500
U – This high-ceilinged, black-and-white-tiled Italian cafe next to the State House is "one of the few updated food options on Beacon Hill"; service can be slow, but the people-watching at lunch is fine, and the pastas and simple Italian entrees can be, too; an "undiscovered" jewel.

Black Rose/SM | 11 | 11 | 12 | $14 |
160 State St. (next to Faneuil Hall Marketplace, South Bldg.), 742-2286
50 Church St. (bet. Massachusetts Ave. & Brattle St.), Cambridge, 492-8630
U – "Tourist hell", this pair of boisterous Irish bars with "good draft beer" loses locals with its "pre-fab food", though the chowder has its champions; the new Harvard Square branch is called "a real snooze"; it peaks on March 17, but some feel the "St. Patrick's Day proceeds should go into renovations."

Boston | F | D | S | C |

Blacksmith House
Outdoor Cafe
| 16 | 13 | 14 | $12 |

56 Brattle St. (bet. Hilliard & Story Sts.), Cambridge, 354-3036
M – For "delightful outside dining" and "terrific desserts", this Harvard Square coffee shop fills the bill – even though the rest of the menu is forgettable, service can be "snotty" and "earplugs and crash helmets are a must" for the sometimes tumultuous location.

Blue Diner/LM
| 17 | 16 | 15 | $14 |

178 Kneeland St. (South St.), 338-4639
U – Boston's answer to the retro-diner craze, in the art-gallery district near South Station, features "funky" booths and big servings of moderately priced, "good home-cooked food", including the "perfect turkey plate special" served by friendly waiters; brunch is a particular treat.

Bluestone Bistro
| 20 | 12 | 15 | $13 |

1799 Commonwealth Ave. (Chiswick Rd.), Brighton, 254-8309
M – "The best thing to happen to Brighton in years" is most noted for its "great pizzas" and "low-key", "bohemian atmosphere" that most find "fun", but others term "unpleasant"; very few put in a good word for the service, which is best described as "confused."

Blue Wave
| – | – | – | M |

142 Berkeley St. (bet. Stuart St. & St. James Ave.), 424-6711
A California grill with heavy Italian overtones, this Back Bay neighborhood hangout has food that some like a lot and others find unremarkable; almost everyone, however, enjoys the pleasant service, good prices and glass-covered tables with clever sand vignettes inside.

Bnu/SM
| 20 | 19 | 18 | $22 |

123 Stuart St. (near Tremont St.), 367-8405
U – "Unbeatable pre- or post-theater", this Nouvelle Italian Theater District storefront trattoria serves "very good pizza" and pastas in a "hip" room with murals of Italian terraces on its concrete walls; even if there are complaints that its "chefs change like the Boston weather", most agree it has "good food and good value."

Boston | **F** | **D** | **S** | **C** |

Bob the Chef/MX | 19 | 10 | 17 | $14 |
604 Columbus Ave. (near Mass. Ave.), 536-6204
M – Boston's best Soul food, though there's little competition; this South End eatery's neighborhood is chancy and the decor sketchy at best; however, it's the only convenient Boston spot for a fix of fried chicken, ham hocks, ribs and sweet potato pie, and the price is right.

Boca Grande | 20 | 10 | 16 | $10 |
149 First St. (bet. Bent & Rogers Sts.), Cambridge, 354-5550
U – This Mexican with very low prices, across from the new Galleria Mall in East Cambridge, is much more than a "dressed-up Taco Bell" – for one thing, it uses "top-quality ingredients" in its cooked-to-order food; the drawbacks are no table service and a minimal setting.

Boodle's of Boston/SM | 19 | 19 | 19 | $29 |
Back Bay Hilton, 40 Dalton St. (bet. Boylston St. & Huntington Ave.), 266-3537
U – You can choose the kind of wood your steaks and fish are grilled on at this "reliable" restaurant in the Back Bay Hilton, near Symphony Hall; some find it expensive and touristy, but most enjoy the well-spaced tables; "great steaks, no yuppies."

Border Cafe/LSM | 17 | 15 | 14 | $15 |
32 Church St. (Palmer St.), Cambridge, 864-6100
819 Rte. 1 (Lynn Fells Pkwy. exit), Saugus, 233-5308
M – The noise, crowds and slow service ("so packed you wait and wait and scream to be heard") don't keep hungry students away from these formula "Mexican Hard Rocks", because of the big portions of "cheap", "decent" burritos, catfish fingers and so on; as the locations go, "Saugus has it all over Cambridge" – it's cleaner and less crowded.

Boston Sail Loft | 17 | 16 | 16 | $16 |
80 Atlantic Ave. (bet. Commercial Wharf & Lewis Wharf), 227-7250
(also see Cambridge Sail Loft)
U – These squeaky-clean singles hangouts are "good for lunch", though "after 5 it's preppy paradise"; the "only topsiders allowed" ambiance turns some off, as does the emphasis on fried food, but both locations are popular for good "value" and good views.

Boston | F | D | S | C |

Botolph's on Tremont | 20 | 19 | 19 | $23 |
569 Tremont St. (bet. Dartmouth & Clarendon Sts.),
424-8577
U – This "SoHo-style bistro" on South End's restaurant row is an offshoot of a Back Bay standby distinguished by its "reasonable prices for inventive food"; some say the Italian offerings are "just ok", but its "great people-watching" and "casual, light" meals have kept it full.

Boylston's | 16 | 15 | 17 | $22 |
(fka The Steak Place)
1268 Boylston St. (across from the Mall at Chestnut Hill), Chestnut Hill, 734-1200
U – A "catering hall" across from the Mall at Chestnut Hill in a room that "looks like an empty convention hall", this place dishes up unexciting but "decent steak" and "ok barbecue"; inexpensive prices for early-bird specials make it a "favorite."

Brandy Pete's/M | 13 | 9 | 14 | $15 |
267 Franklin St. (Batterymarch St.), 439-4165
U – Businessmen were once loyal to this Downtown lunch institution with its mimeographed menus featuring plain, hearty sandwiches and homey mashed potatoes; now that the "best bartenders have left", no one is enamored of anything but the prices.

Brasserie Les Halles | 19 | 19 | 18 | $28 |
301 Faneuil Hall Marketplace (North Market Bldg.),
227-1272
M – The puzzle about this "little, delicious, attractive" French bistro is that while it's "great for an interview" or "business breakfast" and "good for the money", "nobody's ever here"; it's a "reliable", "underrated" choice for Quincy Market, and one of the only places where you know you'll get a table.

Bridge Street Cafe* | 22 | 19 | 20 | $24 |
10A Bridge St. (Elm St.), S. Dartmouth, 508-994-7200
U – At this South Dartmouth cafe, you'll find some first-rate Continental in an attractive but less than comfortable setting; popular with seniors, at times eating here seems like a "nursing home outing."

Boston | F | D | S | C |

BRISTOL LOUNGE/LSM | 20 | 24 | 22 | $26 |
Four Seasons Hotel, 200 Boylston St. (across from
Public Garden), 338-4400
*U – A "quiet, refined" cafe overlooking the Public
Garden on the ground floor of the Four Seasons hotel;
its light meals, piano music, soothing club chairs and
"lovely teas" served from tea carts by liveried waiters
make this a "wonderful place to unwind"; the weekend
Viennese dessert buffet is "pricey", but "the city's best."*

Brodie's Cafe* | 18 | 9 | 15 | $15 |
10½ Cowell St. (Peabody Sq.), Peabody, 508-531-2611
*U – This "local hangout" isn't much more than "a
dump", but the grill food's great for what it is – the
steak tips particularly – with portions that are massive
and prices that are "the best."*

Bull & Finch Pub | 14 | 15 | 12 | $15 |
84 Beacon St. (bet. Arlington & Charles Sts.), 227-9608
*M – TV fans line up behind velvet ropes to see the
original site of "Cheers" – although this dark basement
bar opposite the Public Garden inspired the series, it
doesn't look like the set; "disappointed tourists"
nevertheless leave carrying yellow bags full of souvenirs,
and they sometimes find the burgers "surprisingly good."*

Buoniconti's | 21 | 19 | 20 | $23 |
143 First St. (bet. Binney & Rogers Sts.), Cambridge,
491-3663
*U – This East Cambridge newcomer is a "favorite" for
its "very good", moderately priced Contemporary
Italian food in a "flea-market chic" room; "service has
improved" since opening, and though some say the
food is "indifferent" and comes in "tapas-sized portions",
most consider it a "winner."*

Buster's American Barbecue | – | – | – | I |
1069 Broadway (Rte. 1), Saugus, 233-7100
*Families adore this immense, Western saloon-style joint
with its state-of-the-art BBQ chamber and wonderful
sauce; some Bostonians have even been known to
make the drive out to Saugus just to use the take-out
facilities; prices are low and service cheerful, but it's still
a mass-feeding factory.*

Boston | F | D | S | C |

Buteco/SM | 17 | 10 | 16 | $15 |
130 Jersey St. (near Park Dr. & Boylston St.), 247-9508
57 W. Dedham St. (bet. Tremont & Dartmouth Sts.),
247-9249
U – *"Copious" portions of "el cheapo" Brazilian feijoada and fried yucca, among many other dishes, and a "friendly family atmosphere" keep these neighborhood ethnic standbys ever-popular.*

Cactus Club/LS | 16 | 20 | 15 | $19 |
939 Boylston St. (bet. Boylston & Hereford Sts.), 236-0200
M – *Back Bay "yuppie" bar that's a "frat party with a Tex-Mex theme"; the nachos, fajitas and so on, even if they come in "huge portions", generate few raves – the exuberant Santa Fe-inspired decor, including a smoking stuffed buffalo, is "the best thing about this place."*

Cafe Brazil | 18 | 11 | 18 | $16 |
421 Cambridge St. (near Harvard St.), Allston, 789-5980
U – *This Brazilian newcomer has already attracted a loyal clientele for its "ample portions" of "aromatic and comforting food", served by "very personable waiters" in familiar, if spartan, surroundings.*

CAFE BUDAPEST/SM | 22 | 23 | 22 | $38 |
Copley Hotel, 90 Exeter St. (Huntington Ave.), 266-1979
M – *The grandeur of this "corny but wonderful" "old favorite" is losing its charm for some, who report that its "heavy" and expensive Hungarian food has "gone downhill"; still, the rich cold cherry soup, chicken paprika, goulash and the like still have fans, and many people continue to favor this place for "quiet business meetings" and to "impress people" on special occasions.*

Cafe China/S | 18 | 12 | 16 | $16 |
1245 Cambridge St. (near Hampshire St.), Cambridge, 868-4300
M – *A "happy Eurasian marriage" of Chinese food and Swiss desserts at low prices is the judgment on this Inman Square storefront; although most respondents like the food and "European touches" such as a decent wine list, some say it's "declining."*

Cafe de Paris | 15 | 14 | 11 | $11 |
19 Arlington St. (bet. Newbury & Boylston Sts.), 247-7121
M – *This elegantly paneled cafe facing the Public Garden has much-admired chicken salad and sandwiches served cafeteria-style by young waiters who can seem "snobby", and pastry that "looks better than it tastes"; it's best during a shopping break for a "pricey cup of cappuccino", or to take the kids for an "ice cream fantasy" after a swan boat ride at the Public Garden.*

Boston | F | D | S | C |

Cafe Escadrille | 18 | 17 | 18 | $26 |
26 Cambridge St. (near Rtes. 3A & 128), Burlington, 273-1916

U – An "overpriced and underserviced", "so suburban" Continental, this expense-accounter is an after-work hangout for folks who say it's "good dining for the 'burbs" – faint praise indeed.

Cafe Fleuri/SM | 20 | 21 | 21 | $29 |
Hotel Meridien, 250 Franklin St. (Pearl St.), 451-1900

M – This big French-accented cafe in the atrium of the Hotel Meridien is Downtown "power breakfast heaven"; many deem it Boston's best brunch and enjoy its professional service, but to some the Eclectic fare is "overpriced"; the weekend chocolate buffet is a must for chocolate-lovers.

Cafe Florian/SM | 14 | 15 | 14 | $17 |
85 Newbury St. (bet. Berkeley & Clarendon Sts.), 247-6600

M – A standby for shopping breaks and people-watching on Newbury Street, this Eclectic cafe irritates many reviewers with its "rude" service, "indifferent" food and "dark and dingy" room; still, others appreciate it as a convenient respite if you can get an outdoor table.

Cafe Marliave | 17 | 15 | 17 | $20 |
10 Bosworth St. (bet. Tremont & Provence Sts.), 423-6340

U – An "old, old favorite" Downtown near Filene's, serving Southern Italian food in North End-style surroundings, this institution may turn out food that's "heavy" and "bland", but it's "consistent", and the waiters are pleasant and "reliable."

Cafe Paradiso/SM | 17 | 13 | 14 | $13 |
255 Hanover St. (bet. Cross & Richmond Sts.), 742-1768
1 Eliot Place (Harvard Sq.), Cambridge, 868-3240

U – Twin Italian cafes, one in the North End and one in Harvard Square, with small mirror-topped tables and "excellent coffee"; though they have sandwiches and salads, they're best for late-night cappuccino, cake and "great" gelato.

Cafe Promenade/SM | 18 | 18 | 18 | $24 |
Colonnade Hotel, 120 Huntington Ave. (W. Newton St.), 424-7000

U – This expensive Continental hotel coffee shop at the Colonnade survives on tourists and the pre-Symphony Hall trade, but is also popular for brunch; a recent renovation should raise decor ratings.

| **Boston** | F | D | S | C |

Cafe Rose*
| 13 | 7 | 13 | $15 |

59 Mt. Auburn St. (Stuart St.), Watertown, 924-5401
M – "If you like kebabs", this Watertown Persian may fill a local culinary gap, though the kebab-resistant find it "different but not necessarily delicious" and there are complaints about rudeness.

Cafe Rouge/LSM
| 14 | 15 | 15 | $22 |

Park Plaza Hotel, 50 Park Plaza (bet. Park Sq. & Arlington St.), 426-2000, ext. 352
M – A "glorified coffee shop", this "overpriced" American is known for its "tired" pink decor and "only fair" food; still, it's convenient, especially for breakfast.

Cafe Suisse/LSM
| 20 | 19 | 20 | $25 |

Lafayette Swissotel, 1 Ave. de Lafayette (Washington St.), 451-2600
U – At this above-average coffee shop at the Lafayette, standard Continental fare gives way to frequent festivals of various European regions; it's reliable for meals before performances at the Opera House and a "good place to attempt to civilize children."

Caffe Lampara
| – | – | – | M |

916 Commonwealth Ave. (bet. St. Paul's & Prospect Sts.), Brookline, 566-0300
The popularity of this fun, noisy, loud hangout has a lot to do with its goofy, kitschy decor and its quick, friendly service; the Italian kitchen can get sloppy, but it can also score.

Caffe Luna/SM
| 19 | 17 | 16 | $18 |

Chestnut Hill Star Market Shopping Ctr., 11 Boylston St. (near Rte. 9), Brookline, 734-8400
U – A surprisingly urban Northern Italian trattoria in Chestnut Hill, this spot is most popular for its "designer pizza", appetizers and dessert, either for lunch or before and after the movies; despite some complaints, most people are delighted to have this resource in the neighborhood.

Caffe Vittoria/LSMX
| 20 | 19 | 16 | $12 |

294 Hanover St. (near Prince St.), 227-7606
U – What a Little Italy cafe should be is here in the heart of the North End – a jukebox with Dean Martin and "Volare", a lively crowd, "great cannoli and cappuccino", and granita (a slushy Italian drink) in the summer are among the things that make it "worth the cramped seating."

Boston | **F** | **D** | **S** | **C** |

Cajun Yankee | 21 | 10 | 16 | $23 |
1193 Cambridge St. (near Prospect St.), Cambridge, 576-1971
U – Our participants have a love/hate relationship with this Inman Square Cajun "hole-in-the-wall"; the draw is the spicy food, served in big portions; the drawbacks are the hygiene ("bring your own sponge"), sometimes "rude service", "ugly decor", noise and prices; some say it's "living off its reputation."

Callahan's/LSMX | 14 | 9 | 15 | $17 |
100 Needham St. (bet. Rtes. 9 & 128), Newton, 527-0330
M – This steak house, once a chain, hit on a popular formula – big portions of plain food at low prices – but something went wrong; now there's just one location left, in suburban Newton, with a "gloomy interior" and portions that "have shrunk while prices have risen."

Cambridge Sail Loft | 17 | 16 | 16 | $16 |
1 Memorial Dr. (Kendall Sq.), Cambridge, 225-2222
(see review under Boston Sail Loft)

Candleworks | 19 | 19 | 19 | $26 |
72 N. Water St. (near Rte. 18), New Bedford, 508-992-1635
U – Until recently this South Shore "summer spot" amounted to little more than an "uninspired", "just ok" experience; we hear, however, that recent changes in the kitchen have made this New American a place that "should be better known", and make the above ratings perhaps a little too conservative.

Cantares | 15 | 11 | 15 | $19 |
15 Springfield St. (Cambridge St.), Cambridge, 547-6300
U – An unassuming storefront on Inman Square with popular live music, this is a solid bet for "good" Mexican and South American fare at low prices; nothing spectacular, but good for what it is.

Cantin Abruzzi/SMX | 17 | 10 | 16 | $17 |
51 Lincoln St. (off Walnut St.), Newton Highlands, 964-7260
M – This "North End in the suburbs" Southern Italian in Newton Highlands has "inconsistent" food, but remains busy, with long waits on Saturday nights; it's a good value if you've got kids.

Boston | F | D | S | C |

Cantina Italiana | 20 | 14 | 18 | $21 |
346 Hanover St. (bet. North & Bennington Sts.), 723-4577
U – One of the more consistent and likable Northern Italians in the North End "rarely disappoints" with its food; the stuffed mushrooms and "reasonable" prices have earned it a following thouigh some are unmoved by the "New Jersey-inspired decor."

Cao Palace/MX | 19 | 6 | 13 | $11 |
137 Brighton Ave. (near Harvard St.), Allston, 783-2340
U – A Vietnamese fish market and restaurant, this inexpensive Allston spot has won a following for its very fresh fish and "homey", if grungy, surroundings; the service is "friendly" and the customers loyal.

Capucino's/SM | 16 | 14 | 16 | $19 |
1812 Massachusetts Ave. (near Porter Sq.), Cambridge, 547-8228
1370 Beacon St. (Coolidge Corner), Brookline, 731-4848
1114 Beacon St. (Newton Corner), Newton, 527-2440
40A-44 Atlantic Ave., (1/4 mile from Ocean Ave.), Marblehead, 639-2442
M – This North End-style Italian has four locations, of which Brookline is said to be the best by far; that doesn't mean that everyone likes the food, which can be "boring", or the bland decor; however, sometimes there are virtues to offering "no surprises", especially when prices are low and good garlic bread "unlimited."

Carlo Marino's Ristorante*/S | 21 | 19 | 24 | $23 |
8 Prince St. (bet. Hanover St. & North Sq.), 523-9109
U – A cut above the rest, this Northern Italian wins points for its food, decor and "personable" service; the only surprise is that the place is so "quiet", given its quality.

Carl's Pagoda/LSMX | 23 | 4 | 15 | $18 |
23 Tyler St. (bet. Kneeland & Beach Sts.), 357-9837
M – Long the "in" spot for "Chinese food to die for", this Chinatown perennial may be slipping; we hear complaints that the waiters are "grumpy" and the prices of the Cantonese food have risen while the quality has at best stayed the same; few complain about the "minimal" decor, which is part of the mystique.

Casa Elena | 15 | 11 | 18 | $17 |
45 Lexington St. (Main St.), Watertown, 926-3222
U – The pleasant owners do the cooking and make customers feel welcome at this neighborhood Watertown "favorite" serving Spanish-Mexican food, especially paella; surroundings are plain and prices low.

Boston | F | D | S | C |

Casa Mexico/SM | 17 | 15 | 16 | $19 |
75 Winthrop St. (JFK St.), Cambridge, 491-4552
M – Harvard Square Mexican that at least tries to be authentic, unlike the competition in the area; for many it's a "good, steady" standby with decent margaritas and excellent salsa at moderate prices, while for others it's "falling down" and cold in winter; either way, it hits the spot "if you need an enchilada fix."

Casa Portugal/SM | 19 | 14 | 19 | $18 |
1200 Cambridge St. (Prospect St.), Cambridge, 491-8880
U – An all-around winner for big portions of "hearty" stews, salt cod dishes and the like, this Portuguese near Inman Square has a "homey", slightly "seedy" atmosphere brightened by "warm, friendly" owners and modest prices.

Casa Romero/M | 20 | 20 | 19 | $23 |
30 Gloucester St. (bet. Commonwealth Ave. & Newbury St.), 536-4341
M – Many preferred this long-popular, upscale, "cozy" Back Bay Mexican before it recently changed hands; now there are complaints that the food is "inconsistent" and overpriced; it does, regardless, have a charming courtyard and ratings that argue for giving the new owners a chance to settle in.

Changsho/LSM | 19 | 20 | 17 | $18 |
1712 Massachusetts Ave. (bet. Linnean & Martin Sts.), Cambridge, 547-6565
U – At this extremely popular Porter Square Chinese, both the decor and the Mandarin-Szechuan food are consistently praised, by consensus the "best in Cambridge", service can be slow, but with such great food at such low prices, you'll hear few complaints.

Charles Restaurant, The | 18 | 15 | 18 | $26 |
75 Chestnut St. (bet. Charles & River Sts.), 523-4477
M – This Beacon Hill North End-style Italian is located on a lovely residential street; while naysayers note the dowdy Yankee decor and call it only a "notch above mediocre", others consider it a "great little secret" with "good burgers."

Boston | F | D | S | C |

Charley's Saloon/LSM | 14 | 14 | 15 | $16 |

284 Newbury St. (Gloucester St.), 266-3000
Mall at Chestnut Hill, Rte. 9 (bet. Hammond Pond Pkwy. & Langley Rd.), Chestnut Hill, 964-1200
South Shore Plaza, 250 Granite St. (off Rte. 128), Braintree, 848-0200
Liberty Tree Mall (near Rte. 128), Danvers, 508-774-5800
U – A "tired chain operation" offering burgers and fajitas at several malls, these are the places to go for formula "instant heritage" decor and "'I'm Bill, your waiter'" service; "factory food" and "turnstile service" pretty well sum up these "cheap meals"; nonetheless, the new Newbury Street location, in a Back Bay mansion, is a stunner.

Charlie's Sandwich Shoppe/MX | 21 | 15 | 18 | $10 |

429 Columbus Ave. (bet. W. Newton & Dartmouth Sts.), 536-7669
U – A South End "breakfast institution" to many, crowds flock here for "especially good" pancakes in flavors such as blueberry, cranberry and banana; it's popular, too, for cheeseburgers and other griddle sandwiches at lunch, as well as for its "homey" atmosphere, which mixes people from all walks of life.

Chart House/SM | 17 | 19 | 17 | $24 |

60 Long Wharf (Atlantic Ave.), 227-1576
M – This branch of a national surf-and-turf chain surprises many respondents – it's "not bad for a chain" – with its handsome nautical decor, "good value" and "pleasant" service that's welcoming to children and old aunts, as well as its view of Boston Harbor.

Chatterley's /SM | 12 | 13 | 13 | $18 |
(fka Tia's)
Marriott Long Wharf Hotel, 200 Atlantic Ave. (Long Wharf), 227-0828
M – Location is key at this hotel-restaurant overlooking Quincy Market, where "outdoor dining is pleasant on a summer evening" (fried clams, french fries, sandwiches); however, for most it's a "waste of time for anything but drinks."

Chau Chow/SX | 23 | 4 | 14 | $14 |

52 Beach St. (bet. Harrison Ave. & Kneeland St.), 426-6266
U – This bargain Chinatown Cantonese was a foodie's secret until it was reviewed; it's still top-notch, with the soups and seafood (salt-baked shrimp, fried squid) especially praised, but as you might expect, lines can be long; some say the "waiters have an attitude" and there's no denying that the surroundings are "grim."

Boston

	F	D	S	C

Chef Chang's House/SM | 19 | 12 | 17 | $16 |

1006 Beacon St. (St. Mary's St.), Brookline, 277-4226
M – The price of success for this Mandarin-Szechuan-Shanghaiese near Kenmore Square has been its decline from "one of the best" to "ordinary"; it's still where most locals head when they don't feel like Chinatown, and many dishes, e.g. the Peking duck and Szechuan green beans, have loyalists; however, watch out for "grease" and MSG.

Chef Chow's House/SM | 18 | 12 | 16 | $16 |

230 Harvard St. (near Coolidge Corner), Brookline, 731-3810
50 Church St. (bet. Massachusetts Ave. & Brattle St.), Cambridge, 492-2469
354 Chestnut Hill Ave. (near Cleveland Circle), Brighton, 566-2275
M – Some prefer this Szechuan archrival to Chef Chang's, although the consensus is that it "loses the Coke vs. Pepsi war"; the Harvard Street location is welcome for its lack of lines; the crispy orange beef is a highlight, the decor a lowlight.

Cherrystones/SM | 15 | 17 | 15 | $24 |

100 Atlantic Ave. (on Commercial Wharf), 367-0300
Intersection of Rtes. 1 & 128, Danvers, 774-3300
M – Locals who try this pricey seafood house near Quincy Market feel burned; "overpriced bad food on waterfront spells tourist" and "awful seafood, great site – what a mismatch!" are typical reactions; the brunch at the Danvers location is, regardless, popular, and the Boston room is pretty.

Chez Jean | 17 | 15 | 18 | $26 |

1 Shepard St. (Mass. Ave., across from Holiday Inn), Cambridge, 354-8980
U – Old-fashioned Cambridge cafe that seems preserved from the early 1960s, when Americans were first discovering Julia Child and French food; step into a time warp and order "competent" duck a l'orange, blanquette de veau and other near-forgotten classics.

CHEZ NOUS | 25 | 20 | 24 | $39 |

147 Huron Ave. (Concord Ave.), Cambridge, 864-6670
U – This Nouvelle French in a Cambridge storefront is "one of the few places left for a good, quiet meal"; chef Elizabeth Fischer has attracted a devoted following for her "simple, light French" fare in an "intimate and romantic" setting; not cheap, but worth the price for a first-class, well-served meal.

Boston | F | D | S | C |

Chili's | 12 | 12 | 13 | $13 |
100 Huntington Ave. (Copley Pl.), 859-0134
114 Mt. Auburn St. (bet. University & Eliot Sts.),
Cambridge, 876-8999
M – People love to bash this "Americanized Mexican" chain ("Ronald McDonald meets Miss Mexico", "Filene's Basement meets Tex-Mex"), but low prices and accessibility keep it crowded, especially with families, some of whom actually like the food.

Ciaobella/LSM | 17 | 17 | 15 | $25 |
240A Newbury St. (Fairfield St.), 536-2626
M – While no longer fashionable, this Newbury Street Northern Italian with its outdoor dining and its stab at a European ambiance remains crowded; "occasionally the food can be very good", but many find it "inconsistent", "bland" and overpriced.

Circle Pizza/SMX | 17 | 7 | 10 | $10 |
361 Hanover St. (Fleet St.), 523-8787
M – This classic North End pizza joint has long been famous for its thick crusts; some say it has gone downhill, but many others still regard it as the best.

Ciro's/SM | 17 | 14 | 17 | $21 |
239 Harvard St. (½ block from Beacon St.), Brookline, 277-7112
M – A so-so suburban Northern Italian that "used to be better", this spot now gathers complaints about slow service and inconsistency; however, partisans of its soft-shell crabs and moderate prices say it's "adorable."

Cityside/LSM | 13 | 13 | 13 | $16 |
Faneuil Hall Marketplace (Quincy Market Bldg.), 742-7390
1960 Beacon St. (Chestnut Hill Ave. at Cleveland Circle), 566-1002
U – At these pick-up bars at Faneuil Hall and Cleveland Circle, there's "not much going on if you're over 21"; the moderate prices, location and outdoor dining keep tourists and students coming, but naysayers call them "Cityclatter" and "dumpster dining."

Claddagh | 10 | 11 | 14 | $15 |
119 Dartmouth St. (Columbus Ave.), 262-9874
U – This "definitely Irish" Back Bay pub is a cheerful place to go "just for the brews", but the "below average" food means that "sometimes it's better to go hungry."

Boston | F | D | S | C |

Clarke's | 16 | 12 | 14 | $15 |
21 Merchant's Row (State St.), 227-7800
U – This Faneuil Hall "after-work social scene" is more "maelstrom" than restaurant, though many find the burgers enjoyable; go to practice your sardine imitation, or to meet a congenial soul.

Club Cafe/LSM | 17 | 18 | 17 | $23 |
209 Columbus Ave. (near Berkeley St.), 536-0966
U – "Chic" South End piano bar serving Eclectic fare to a devoted, largely gay following is nice to look at and has pleasant music, but both the food and service, though respectable, could be improved.

Colorado Public Library/SM | 18 | 20 | 18 | $22 |
10 Brookline Place W. (bet. Rte. 9 & Washington St.), Brookline Village, 734-6772
U – Former resistance to this standby steak house has broken down; now people praise the consistency of the steaks and lamb chops, as well as the "quiet, restful dining" in a room decorated to look like a paneled library; it's good for families.

Commonwealth Brewing Company/SM | 12 | 18 | 13 | $15 |
138 Portland St. (bet. New Chardon & Causeway Sts.), 523-8383
U – "The brew is fabulous" at this working brewery near the Boston Garden, surrounded by barrels and "gleaming copper vats"; the undistinguished nachos, chili and smoked meats exist just to keep the beer and ale going down; it's a "great place before or after a game."

Coolidge Corner Clubhouse | 16 | 15 | 16 | $13 |
307 Harvard St. (bet. Beacon & Babcock Sts.), Brookline, 566-4948
U – This big sports bar and grill in a central Brookline location has hit on a formula that works: "man-size portions" of "great" burgers, sandwiches and onion rings for little money; with the hordes of college kids and the many TVs tuned to sports events, it's "exactly what you expect, but with better food."

Copley's/LSM | 21 | 24 | 21 | $32 |
Copley Plaza Hotel, 138 St. James Ave. (Copley Sq.), 267-5300
M – This recently renovated Back Bay hotel dining room's decor wins praise as "gracious"; the New England regional food, while "better than average", isn't really as much the draw here as the Old Boston atmosphere; for this sort of elegance, the prices are pretty reasonable.

Boston

| F | D | S | C |

CORNUCOPIA
| 24 | 22 | 21 | $31 |

15 West St. (bet. Tremont & Washington Sts.), 338-4600
U – The "imaginative", "well-prepared" Contemporary American menu executed by chef Stuart Cameron at this Downtown restaurant in a historic building has won a delighted following, who enjoy "dining, not eating"; there's a carefully selected wine list and many wines by the glass; it's good "with a new friend" or for lunch while shopping.

Cornwall's/LSM
| 18 | 16 | 17 | $16 |

510 Commonwealth Ave. (Kenmore Sq.), 262-3749
U – A "cozy" English-style pub in Kenmore Square combines an "outstanding beer selection" with ambitious food at reasonable prices; those who go say it's a "great find", especially good before a game at Fenway.

Cottonwood Cafe/S
| 20 | 21 | 18 | $25 |

1815 Massachusetts Ave. (Porter Sq.), 661-7440
M – This tremendously popular Southwestern cafe features eye-catching mock-Santa Fe decor; although there are complaints about the lines and the prices, everyone loves the "superb" margaritas and enjoys "all the Southwestern basics" on the menu.

Cricket's/SM
| 15 | 15 | 14 | $19 |

Faneuil Hall Marketplace (South Market Bldg.), 720-5570
U – Exposed brick and ferns are the basic motifs at this Faneuil Hall bar-restaurant, where the people-watching, drinks and music are all fine, but the traditional American menu is "predictable."

Dad's Beantown Diner/L
| 11 | 17 | 14 | $14 |

911 Boylston St. (bet. Hereford & Gloucester Sts.), 296-3237
U – At this moderately priced Back Bay mock-'50s diner, they "need to improve everywhere but decor"; BU students go because it's open late and it's well-located; our surveyors' final verdict: "good concept, not-so-good food."

Daily Catch/SMX
| 22 | 12 | 16 | $20 |

323 Hanover St. (bet. Little Prince & Richmond Sts.), 523-8567
261 Northern Ave. (adjacent to Boston Fish Pier), 338-3093
219 Elm St. (Davis Sq.), Somerville, 623-0375
U – Calamari and garlic in quantity account for the popularity of these small, forever-packed places, where you sit at little tables and have fish brought to you in the frying pan; the "novelty wears off if you go too often", but if you've got visitors or need a squid fix, it's great fun; the monkfish marsala is winning fans, too.

Boston | **F** | **D** | **S** | **C** |

Dakota's/S | 19 | 21 | 19 | $28 |
34 Summer St. (Arch St.), 737-1777
U – Decorated with opulent red granite, this big, trendy Contemporary American steak house in the Downtown Financial District is busy and "loud" at lunch, but dinner is sparsely attended because the area is so quiet at night; happy hour, with "good free hors d'oeuvre", is a safe bet.

DALI | 24 | 21 | 21 | $24 |
415 Washington St. (near Beacon St.), 661-3254
U – This Cambridge tapas bar near Inman Square caught on immediately for its festive atmosphere, "genuinely warm and friendly" staff and "wonderful" tapas "for garlic lovers"; the sangria and extensive Spanish wine list are also much admired; even if the entrees are less memorable, it "fills a huge void for good Spanish food in Boston."

Da Natale* | 25 | 24 | 23 | $23 |
448 Hanover St. (near Commercial St.), 720-4480
U – A true sleeper, this North End Italian's "big portions" of "wonderful, fresh, fragrant" cooking ought to be better known; the "friendly, family-like service" and "quiet, romantic" room are pluses, too.

DAVIDE/SM | 24 | 20 | 22 | $34 |
326 Commercial Ave. (across from Union Wharf), 227-5745
U – Though this fancy Northern Italian is just a little outside the North End, it's far above it in terms of ambition and delivery; although a vocal minority find it "pretentious" and pricey, most admire its "elegance", exemplary service and "dependable", excellent food.

DAVIO'S/SM | 23 | 19 | 20 | $28 |
269 Newbury St. (bet. Fairfield & Gloucester Sts.), 262-4810
Hotel Sonesta, 5 Cambridge Pkwy. (across from Cambridgeside Galleria), Cambridge, 661-4810
204 Washington St. (off Rte. 9), Brookline, 738-4810
U – An extremely popular pair of Nuova Cucina Italians in Back Bay and Brookline Village with a new addition in Cambridge, these siblings win praise for their consistency and "classy settings"; most prefer the Brookline location, but recommend the upstairs cafe on Newbury Street for quick and good pizzas at moderate prices; service can be slow.

Boston

| F | D | S | C |

Demo's Restaurant | 19 | 4 | 15 | $13 |
64 Mt. Auburn St. (bet. Summer & Main Sts.),
Watertown, 924-9660
U – Greek lamb and other dishes served in big, "bargain-priced" portions draw a devoted following to this Watertown hole-in-the-wall; the shish kebab is very "tasty" and "kids love" the food.

Division Sixteen/LSM | 17 | 14 | 13 | $16 |
955 Boylston St. (bet. Hereford St. & Mass. Ave.),
353-0870
U – The "sexual energy and food don't mix" for some at this "noisy" Back Bay meet-market in a former police station, but many others love the burgers, nachos and buffalo wings, all served in "mammoth quantities"; service can be "non-existent", but fans still consider the place "fun"; delivery service, with their fleet of trucks, is amazingly efficient.

Dockside | 14 | 13 | 13 | $14 |
183 State St. (Atlantic Ave.), 723-7050
U – Forgettable bar food steps up to the plate at this sports pub near Faneuil Hall; it's good for a "casual drink", but most people go to places like this to root, not forage.

Domenico's* | 23 | 16 | 19 | $18 |
356 Bennington St. (bet. Bremen & Chelsea Sts.), East
Boston, 567-8300
U – Fans say the moderately priced Italian food at this East Boston spot is as good as or better than any in the North End, and waits are shorter than you often face on the other side of the tunnel; "good veal dishes" come in for special praise.

Donatello's | 22 | 21 | 22 | $29 |
444 Broadway (Rte. 1 North), Saugus, 233-9975
U – Recommended for "well-prepared" Northern Italian food outside the city, this restaurant has all the elements, from a "lovely bar" to "classic service" – no wonder it's so popular; the only serious complaint is that it's "expensive for Saugus", but after all, "you get what you pay for."

Dom's/SM | 20 | 15 | 20 | $28 |
100 Bartlett Place (Salem & Parmenter Sts.), 523-9279
U – One of Boston's phoenixes, this North End Italian "holds its own" against newer competition by virtue of its "very good" food and the "nice people" who greet you; perhaps pricey, but fans point out it's "always good."

Boston

| F | D | S | C |

Dover Sea Grille/SM | 20 | 19 | 19 | $26 |
1223 Beacon St. (St. Paul St.), Brookline, 566-7000
M – Most find this dressy – some say "stuffy" – seafood restaurant in a former hotel lobby a "great second choice" to Legal; although it's only a bit more expensive, you can make reservations and enjoy the "privacy" of widely spaced tables; it's a reliable place to take dates and visiting parents, with food that's "always satisfying."

D.R. Brown's* | 14 | 12 | 14 | $12 |
1010 Beacon St. (bet. St. Mary's & Carlton Sts.), Brookline, 566-5983
M – Formerly Brown's Steak House, this perennial "local hangout" has moved to smaller quarters a few doors nearer Fenway Park; the old location is missed, but people who still want to load up on low-priced beef and other "mostly heavy food" before a game find their way here.

Du Barry*/SM | 15 | 14 | 16 | $25 |
159 Newbury St. (near Dartmouth St.), 262-2445
M – Those who have come to this Classic French on Newbury Street over the years find it "always ordinary, but reassuring in a funny way"; other than its survival, however, there's not much to impress; a recently added greenhouse is pleasant, and the omelettes and pommes frites have their fans, but many are "disappointed."

Durgin Park | – | – | – | M |
Faneuil Hall Marketplace (North Market Bldg.), 227-2038
Nothing ever changes at this venerable dining hall, where the help delights in slamming gargantuan slabs of roast beef on the table and cracking wise to customers; the New England regional menu, featuring lobster, baked beans and Indian pudding, has stayed the same for decades, as have the long serving tables and longer lines of tourists, who have good reasons for loving this place.

Dynasty/SM | 18 | 14 | 14 | $15 |
33 Edinboro St. (near Beach St.), 350-7777
U – You can have a "quiet" lunch in above-average surroundings at this large Chinatown emporium; though service is friendly, surveyors' enthusiasm is reserved mostly for the "very good" dim sum at very reasonable prices.

Boston | F | D | S | C |

Eagle Brook Saloon* | 14 | 13 | 14 | $18 |
258 Dedham St. (Rtes. 1A & 115), Norfolk, 508-384-7312
M – At this Traditional American, many love the "bare and exotic decor" that resembles a Western saloon, complete with swinging doors, as well as the immense portions; however, most say this "dark, dreary" dive is "not worth going to", and that while prices are cheap, they're still "expensive for what you get."

EAST COAST GRILL/SM | 24 | 16 | 19 | $24 |
1271 Cambridge St. (near Prospect St.), Cambridge, 491-6568
U – This elemental Inman Square storefront "delivers exactly what it promises" – "the best BBQ in Boston" and "fantastic", Caribbean-influenced dishes, all served by chef-owner Chris Schlesinger and an "exceptionally friendly staff"; the no-reservations policy often means waiting for a long time in close, noisy quarters; but whether you're in "black tie or jeans", the place is "the greatest"; P.S. the restaurant has a "perfect" takeout, Jake & Earl's, next door.

Eastern Pier Seafood | – | – | – | M |
237 Atlantic Ave. (Fish Pier), 423-7756
With the same owners as Chau Chow, this waterside haven for Chinese seafood matches its sibling for top-quality, very fresh seafood and lightning-quick service (don't order everything at once unless you want it to arrive all at once); the only differences are a bar and a little more formality.

Elsie's/LSMX | 15 | 6 | 13 | $9 |
71A Mt. Auburn St. (Holyoke St.), Cambridge, 354-8781
M – A "Harvard landmark" that some call "tarnished" and others a "great institution", this stand-up sandwich shop "brings back memories of my youth" for those who have lined up over the years for its roast beef specials; however, without the nostalgia, the "huge" sandwiches with "fatty" meat may not taste as good.

Emilio's | 18 | 10 | 17 | $21 |
361 Hanover St. (Clark St.), 367-2246
M – A "typical North End" Italian with a highly visible Hanover Street location, this spot's regulars complain that a recent change of menu "caters to tourists"; nonetheless, the "dependable" mussel and veal dishes receive high marks.

Boston | **F** | **D** | **S** | **C** |

Ethiopian Restaurant/SM | 15 | 9 | 16 | $14 |

333 Massachusetts Ave. (Huntington Ave.), 247-7204
M – This family-run restaurant with bright white laminated walls began a vogue for Ethiopian food in Boston; some find the stews and homemade pancakes, which are torn and used as utensils, "unique and welcome", and compliment the "gracious" service; others find the food oily and say "once is enough"; N.B. it's said to have "improved recently."

European Restaurant/LSM | 15 | 9 | 14 | $15 |

218 Hanover St. (bet. Cross & Parmenter Sts.), 523-5694
M – A huge "tourist factory" in a prominent North End location, the Italian menu here is as long as your arm, and critics think it should be kept at arm's length; go "just for the pizza", which has a significant number of sincere fans; however, one disappointed diner says it's the "first restaurant you see and the last you want to be found in."

Fajita Rita's | 15 | 10 | 13 | $12 |

25 West St. (bet. Tremont & Washington Sts.), 426-1222
U – At this bustling Downtown storefront they "try hard" and succeed at fajitas and a few other simple Mexican specialties, all at low prices; go for a quick and lively lunch, but skip dinner – it closes early and the neighborhood dies at night.

Felicia's/SM | 18 | 15 | 17 | $23 |

145A Richmond St. (bet. Hanover & North Sts.), 523-9885
M – This North End standby has seen better days, when the celebrities whose photographs line the staircase regularly came for cannelloni; now it's "dark and gloomy", with surveyors unimpressed by "arrogant" waiters and food "drowning in red sauce"; still, a persistent minority finds it "underrated."

57 Restaurant/LSM | 17 | 16 | 18 | $27 |

Howard Johnson's Hotel, 200 Stuart St. (near Park Sq.), 423-5700
M – The only thing reviewers agree on is that this hotel-restaurant serving "basic" American food is convenient for a night at the theater; the roast beef can be either "great" or "awful", the food "surprisingly fine" or "like leftovers", the service "good" or "erratic", decor "very comfortable" or "stuffy"; more than most, this spot is a matter of timing and taste.

| Boston | F | D | S | C |

Finally Michael's | 17 | 17 | 18 | $25 |
2108 Worcester Rd. (Rte. 9 West), Framingham, 508-237-6180
M – Some feel this Contemporary American is "nothing extraordinary" and "overpriced" to boot; however, its partisans cite its "pleasant atmosphere" that's reminiscent of a library, its "great early-bird dinner specials" and a better-than-average salad bar.

Five North Square | 20 | 18 | 19 | $25 |
5 North Sq. (bet. North Sq. and Prince St.), 720-1050
U – An ambitious North End Italian with "pretty", "romantic" decor, this "true jewel" tries to provide "attentive and courteous" service and lighter, more elegant food than the area's norm; most think they succeed, but a few find it overpriced.

FIVE SEASONS/S | 24 | 16 | 20 | $22 |
669A Centre St. (bet. Severns Ave. & Green St.), Jamaica Plain, 524-9016
U – For "homey, healthy vegetarian" food, turn to this Jamaica Plain storefront with wooden tables and long lines; even though prices can be higher than you'd expect, the portions are big, and regulars "love this kooky place."

FLASH IN THE PAN | 25 | 16 | 21 | $27 |
181 Newbury St. (bet. Rtes. 114 & 62), Danvers, 508-774-9367
U – An unlikely spot for "a true dining experience" is this '50s-style diner that turns out "outstanding" Contemporary American dishes, most notably "duck worth driving from anywhere for"; it's "a place one doesn't want to get popular", especially if one is local.

Florence's Restaurant/SM | 21 | 13 | 18 | $20 |
190 North St. (Richmond St.), 523-4480
U – Major quantities of "solid red-sauce Italian" food at moderate prices, served with "no pretense" in plain but "homey" surroundings, are the stock-in-trade of this North End fixture; it's "not fancy, just very good."

Freestones | 14 | 16 | 16 | $20 |
41 William St. (N. 2nd St.), New Bedford, 508-993-7477
U – A "noisy, crowded" "pick-up joint" that just happens to have "the best clam chowder" in the area, this seafoodery is "tolerable, and better than starving to death", but ultimately no great shakes.

Boston | F | D | S | C |

Frogg Lane Bar & Grille/SM | 13 | 14 | 13 | $15 |
Faneuil Hall Marketplace (Quincy Market Bldg.), 720-0610
M – This Faneuil Hall formula bar's nachos and burgers are best avoided, say most of our reviewers; it's strictly "for tourists on a budget" who are not meticulous.

Fuddruckers | 13 | 9 | 10 | $10 |
8 Park Pl. (Stuart St.), 723-3833
U – Part of a Texas-style chain, this Theater District joint is good only for burgers served with many toppings; it may be cheap, but some surveyors would just as soon "close 'em up."

Galeria Umberto/MX | 21 | 10 | 13 | $7 |
289 Hanover St. (bet. Richmond & Prince Sts.), 523-9261
U – A big open hall with Formica tables in the heart of the North End, this inexpensive Italian draws sizable crowds at lunch for the "best" pizza and calzone, and arancine (rice croquettes) "to die for"; open only during the day.

Gardner Museum Cafe/SMX | 18 | 19 | 15 | $16 |
280 The Fenway (next to Simmons College), 566-1088
U – A "tiny retreat for tired feet" at a treasured museum, this "relaxing" spot features soups, sandwiches and salads (at lunch only) served in "generous portions"; it's perfect for a bite after taking in the art, there's outdoor seating in good weather and wherever you sit it's "n-i-c-e."

Genji/SM | 20 | 18 | 18 | $24 |
327 Newbury St. (bet. Hereford St. & Mass. Ave.), 267-5656
M – The "first fancy Japanese in Boston", this Back Bay perennial is still popular for its "very good" sushi and for "pleasant, serene meals"; however, it's expensive and some say it has "slipped", with decor "getting stale" and service "slow."

GIACOMO'S/S | 24 | 16 | 22 | $22 |
355 Hanover St. (bet. Little Prince & Fleet Sts.), 523-9026
U – Those who know this North End Italian with its open kitchen are crazy about the "excellent" and moderately priced seafood, which "rivals the Daily Catch", as well as the "excellent, schmaltzy" (though sometimes "rushed") service; it's "small and fun" and often crowded.

Boston | F | D | S | C |

Giannino's/S | 17 | 16 | 16 | $26 |
20 University Rd. (Charles Hotel Courtyard), 661-0733
U – *An upscale North End-style Italian at Charles Square, the mall at Harvard Square, this spot is invariably calm and pleasant, but pricey; moreover, the food doesn't generate much excitement: "everything seems right – so why is it so forgettable?"*

Gill's Grill | 17 | 16 | 16 | $24 |
157 Turnpike Rd. (2 miles from Westboro exit, Massachusetts Turnpike), Westboro, 508-366-7993
M – *"A litle bit of San Francisco in Metro West", this California-inspired restaurant's fans say it "takes chances and succeeds", while foes consider it a "disappointment"; it's your roll of the dice.*

Goemon/S | 17 | 15 | 16 | $14 |
1 Kendall Place, Bldg. 100 (Hampshire & Cardinal Medeiros Sts.), Cambridge, 577-9595
M – *At this sleek, Japanese-style noodle shop at Kendall Square, you design your own steaming bowl of soup from a long list of ingredients (there are other light Japanese meals, too); the price is right and the concept novel, but service is "erratic."*

Golden Palace/LSM | 20 | 13 | 14 | $16 |
14 Tyler St. (bet. Beach & Kneeland Sts.), 423-4565
U – *Many of our voters have had the "best dim sum in Boston" at this big banquet hall in Chinatown, which tore out the Polynesian trappings of the old Bob Lee's Islander; the dim sum carts are wheeled around every day from 9 AM to 3 PM, but "everyone goes on Sunday", when waits can be long.*

Golden Temple/LSM | 17 | 18 | 17 | $17 |
1651 Beacon St. (Washington Sq.), Brookline, 277-9722
U – *Centrally located in suburban Brookline, this Chinese standby's recent renovation with Italian-style furniture has wowed locals, who cite a "vast improvement" both in the Chinese-Polynesian food and in the service; luckily the prices didn't go up when the new decor did.*

Gourmeli's | 15 | 15 | 16 | $22 |
Marriott Copley Plaza, 110 Huntington St. (Copley Pl.), 236-5800
M – *A Marriott room that's by most accounts a misfire – our raters find the American menu "stereotypical" and "standard", and sometimes worse; the clam chowder and the weekend buffets have their fans, but there's little enthusiasm for this place.*

Boston

| F | D | S | C |

Grape Vine* | 22 | 17 | 22 | $22 |
26 Congress St. (across from Alden Merrell), Salem, 508-745-9335
U – A "warm feeling" pervades this "casual", "well-done" North Shore Italian that's "trying hard"; although in terms of atmosphere it's "nicer at night", the lunch prices are a "best buy."

Great Stuff | 19 | 12 | 14 | $12 |
Faneuil Hall Marketplace (Center Bldg.), 720-7883
The Atrium, Rte. 9 (near Rte. 128), Newton, 969-1495
M – Not so great stuff – at both prime locations, we hear complaints of "tired" salads and sandwiches, and that even the minimal, cafeteria-style service can be slow; still, many figure it's fine for a "lunch on the run"; the Quincy Market location has no seating.

GREEN STREET GRILL/S | 23 | 11 | 18 | $21 |
280 Green St. (bet. Magazine & Pearl Sts.), Cambridge, 876-1655
U – This "great dive" behind Central Square has "innovative", "spectacularly well-prepared" Caribbean food, especially the sausages so hot they can "make your ears water"; however, most love the burn as much as they do chef John Levins, who is a "sorcerer"; all in all, "the best dump in Cambridge."

Grendel's Den/SM | 12 | 13 | 13 | $15 |
89 Winthrop St. (JFK St.), Cambridge, 491-1050
U – Everything's funky about this prototypical Harvard Square institution, where the housekeeping could use a hand; the variety at the salad bar and the low prices keep this "'60s flashback" going strong.

GRILL 23/SM | 22 | 21 | 21 | $36 |
161 Berkeley St. (Stuart St.), 542-2255
U – The "best steak in town" to some is served in this clubby, "masculine" Back Bay room; the people-watching's great, even if the high ceilings make it so noisy that it's "like eating inside a drum"; despite complaints about prices, especially on the wine list, the staff is "well-trained", and you "can't go wrong taking a client or your boss."

G'Vanni's/LSM | 19 | 16 | 17 | $28 |
2 Prince St. (bet. North Sq. & Hanover St.), 523-0107
M – This small, precious North End Italian is known for its whimsical decor, closely spaced tables and "old-style" food that some say has gone "downhill" while prices have gone up; a draw is door-to-door limo service for parties of more than four – best booked in advance.

Boston

| F | D | S | C |

Gyosai*
| 18 | 12 | 18 | $25 |

Faneuil Hall Marketplace Center, 200 State St. (Surface Rd.), 345-0942
U – *A very large selection of sushi and other Japanese dishes is a strength of this new, well-liked, elemental Japanese at Faneuil Hall; businessmen appreciate the short waits at lunch, and those who have discovered it enjoy the "very fresh" sushi.*

GYUHAMA /LSM
| 24 | 18 | 19 | $24 |

827 Boylston St. (bet. Gloucester & Fairfield Sts.), 437-0188
U – *Boston's Top Japanese specializes in the "best sushi" and "freshest sashimi" in town; the decor at the Back Bay basement is functional, if less than exceptional, and the service is "sometimes not attentive", but that doesn't concern the sushi addicts who come in droves; it's open until 2 AM during the week.*

HAMERSLEY'S BISTRO/SM
| 26 | 18 | 22 | $36 |

578 Tremont St. (bet. Clarendon & Dartmouth Sts.), 267-6068
U – *"Really sensational" Eclectic food on a French base has made this South End storefront "as close to a real bistro as you can get in Boston"; chef Gordon Hamersley "gets better all the time without being pretentious about his food"; no matter what, he keeps the lemon-garlic roasted chicken, many people's favorite dish, on the menu; the small tables are "cramped" and some "wish it were cheaper", but customers generally feel they get their money's worth.*

Hampshire House/SM
| 18 | 22 | 19 | $30 |

84 Beacon St. (across from Public Garden), 227-9600
M – *Much of the crowd at this Classic American, on Beacon Hill by the Public Garden, is drawn by Cheers, the downstairs pub; though respectable, the food upstairs "doesn't compare with prices and atmosphere", which is a shame, because people like the "old-time Boston ambiance" at Sunday brunch.*

Hanmiok*
| 18 | 8 | 15 | $12 |

351 Washington St. (Market St.), 783-2090
U – *An unassuming Brighton storefront houses this lovely and "very authentic" Japanese-Korean; the prices are great, the sushi and tempura first-rate and it's still relatively undiscovered.*

Boston | F | D | S | C |

Happy Haddock/MX | 18 | 10 | 14 | $13 |
Wellington Shopping Center, 491 Riverside Ave.
(Wellington Circle), Medford, 395-3222
U – With fish served cafeteria-style at low prices, it's no surprise that this seafoodery is astoundingly popular; you're better off avoiding the six o'clock rush, when a crush of families come for the "no frills" food served by "friendly people."

Hard Rock Cafe/LS | 15 | 21 | 15 | $16 |
131 Clarendon St. (bet. Columbus & Boylston Sts.),
424-7625
M – Come prepared for hordes of tourists, deafening noise, high prices for hearty hamburgers and T-shirts that cost as much as your meal; there's no fighting the lure for young teenagers of this national chain-cum-rock 'n' roll museum, so bring earplugs, tranquilizers and lots of cash.

Harvard Bookstore Cafe/SM | 17 | 16 | 15 | $17 |
190 Newbury St. (bet. Dartmouth & Exeter Sts.),
536-0095
M – This popular bookstore on Newbury Street offers dining at all hours, but is best in nice weather, when you can sit outdoors and people-watch; since Moncef Meddeb, the founder of L'Espalier, designed a menu with grilled meats and salads inspired by his native Tunisia, the food has been "much improved"; still-slow service draws complaints.

Harvard Gardens | 10 | 6 | 13 | $14 |
310-320 Cambridge St. (bet. Grove & Charles Sts.),
523-2727
U – A "grubby standby" where Mass General workers and sports fans en route to or from the Garden get "cheap, decent" hamburgers, this "dark" room "hasn't changed in 30 years"; in sum, it's an "if you're in the immediate vicinity and it's raining" sort of place.

HARVARD STREET GRILL/L | 25 | 17 | 22 | $32 |
398 Harvard St. (bet. Naples & Fuller Sts.), Brookline,
734-9834
U – "One of the best kept secrets" in town, this Brookline storefront offers nearly "perfect" Eclectic food with a French accent, cooked by chef-owner John Vyhanek, with lamb chops and desserts especially outstanding; the plain room isn't up to the cooking, and the prices are too high for regulars to be as regular as they'd like, but reviewers say "this never disappoints" and hope it isn't "too good to last."

Boston | F | D | S | C |

Harvest/SM | 21 | 18 | 18 | $32 |
44 Brattle St. (near Mt. Auburn St.), Cambridge, 492-1115
M – A Harvard institution, this Contemporary American's glory days may be gone, but fans still consider it the only serious restaurant around; critics complain of small portions at large prices and wonder when the "musty" Marimekko-print decor will be renovated, or whether the owners plan to keep it as a museum of the early '70s; the cafe is cheaper, and also serves the house's "wonderful" bread.

Hilltop Steak House | 19 | 10 | 16 | $18 |
855 Broadway (Rte. 1), Saugus, 233-7700
M – This "cow palace" still "packs 'em in" despite steaks that are sometimes great, sometimes disappointing, and a "herd 'em in, herd 'em out" attitude toward diners, with long waits being commonplace; even with its famous lobster pie, amusingly tacky atmosphere and extremely "fair prices", there's "no real enjoyment" for many.

Houlihan's/SM | 14 | 14 | 14 | $16 |
60 State St. (near Faneuil Hall), 367-6377
U – Part of a "yuppie food chain", this formula fern-bar dishes out "bland and boring" burgers, steaks and fajitas; the bar, with many televisions tuned to sports events, is a popular place to "hang"; while not great, this place is "sturdy."

House of Siam/SM | 19 | 14 | 17 | $17 |
21 Huntington Ave. (near Exeter St.), 267-1755
M – Conveniently located at Copley Square, this Thai's simple decor and "good" spicy specialties have earned it a certain following, although some deem it just "middle of the road."

Ho Yuen Ting Seafood/SMX | 22 | 6 | 14 | $15 |
13A Hudson St. (bet. Beach & Kneeland Sts.), 426-2316
58 Beach St. (Tyler St.), 426-2341
U – The "best Hong Kong-style seafood in Boston" can now be found at two Chinatown locations around the corner from each other, with the original on Hudson Street preferred; neither has any decor, but the service is friendly and the whole steamed fish and spicy squid are "not to be missed."

Hungry I/SM | 22 | 20 | 21 | $33 |
71½ Charles St. (bet. Mt. Vernon & Revere Sts.), 227-3524
U – There's "charm galore" at this tiny downstairs Beacon Hill Contemporary American, where good waiters serve "imaginative" game and other dishes to couples who dote on the "quaint", "utterly romantic" atmosphere; a few quibble with the prices.

Boston | F | D | S | C |

ICARUS/S | 24 | 24 | 22 | $37 |
3 Appleton St. (bet. Arlington & Berkeley Sts.), 426-1790
U – *An elegant South End secret, this New American garners many raves for its "delicious, imaginative" food, its tastefully eclectic dining room and its "friendly", professional service – all in all, a restaurant ripe for discovery; a handful of critics find it "disappointing" and "overpriced."*

IL CAPRICCIO | 25 | 16 | 22 | $37 |
53 Prospect St. (bet. Vermont & Charles Sts.), Waltham, 894-2234
U – *"The chef really takes pride in the food, and it shows" at this "always enjoyable" Northern Italian; not that there aren't quibbles – the "small space" is a problem and the staff, while "personable", tends to "play up to regulars" – but the "A+ food" goes a long way toward justifying the expense.*

Il Dolce Momento/LSMX | 15 | 11 | 10 | $11 |
30 Charles St. (near Chestnut St.), 720-0477
U – *This "late-night gelati spot" "could only survive on Charles Street" – though the gelato's "super", all else is "poor", from the "very loud and always smoky" room to the wait staff that appears to be "brain-dead."*

Imperial Tea House/LSM | 18 | 10 | 14 | $15 |
70 Beach St. (Hudson St.), 426-8439
U – *Short on atmosphere but long on popularity, this Chinatown spot is best known for "great dim sum", "cheap, filling and good"; though the rest of the menu is "basic" and the service is "variable", the restaurant bustles during the weekend brunching hours; "come early to avoid lines."*

India Pavilion | 22 | 11 | 16 | $16 |
17 Central Square (near Mass. Ave.), Cambridge, 547-7463
U – *A "longtime favorite" for "excellent", "authentic" Indian cuisine, this tiny, crowded Cambridge standby's decor strikes some as "tacky" and the service as sometimes "hostile"; nonetheless, it's unquestionably the "best Indian in town" – and a great value.*

Iruna/MX | 18 | 12 | 17 | $19 |
56 JFK St. (near Mt. Auburn St.), Cambridge, 868-5633
M – *This "Harvard Square classic" gets mixed reviews for the quality of its Spanish food (everything from "boring" to "great"), but it's "comfy and reliable", with a "lovely" garden setting and lots of "old-world charm"; generous portions and "incredibly reasonable" prices make it a "nice place for a cheap date."*

Boston | F | D | S | C |

Jacob Wirth/SM | 13 | 15 | 14 | $18 |

31 Stuart St. (near Tremont St.), 338-8586
M – This Theater District "time machine" may be "past its prime", but it's still widely regarded as a fun place for sausage and a beer – especially the dark draft variety; the plank floors, "lovely old" paneling and German "he-man" food are all reasonably authentic, but many surveyors feel that JW is surviving mainly on reputation and location.

Jae's Cafe and Grill | – | – | – | I |

520 Columbus Ave. (Concord Sq. & Worcester St.), 421-9405
This Korean with a health-food twist would probably be better known were it not tucked away in a little South End neighborhood; it's a shame, because its small but pleasant outdoor area and winning service make it "a jewel."

JASPER'S/M | 26 | 23 | 25 | $48 |

240 Commercial St. (Atlantic Ave., across from Lewis Wharf), 523-1126
U – Chef-owner Jasper White has been the king of Boston chefs for a decade; maintaining his touch for "outstanding" updated New England food, especially impeccable seafood, he has brought down his prices – they're now lower than the Survey reflects, which qualifies this as an authentic dining bargain; he's also redecorated, and the bold new colors are striking.

J.C. Hillary's Ltd./SM | 15 | 15 | 16 | $17 |

793 Boylston St. (near Fairfield St.), 536-6300
985 Providence Hwy. (Rte. 1 So.), Dedham, 329-0800
311 Mishawum Rd. (near Rte. 95), Woburn, 935-7200
55 Boston Post Rd. (Rte. 20W), Wayland, 508-358-5124
M – Outposts of an anonymous, cheerful fern-bar chain, these spots are fine for "good burgers" and popular "light items" that make reliably quick lunches at moderate prices; detractors complain there's "no substance", but most think they're "good for what they are"; the Woburn location is considered the best.

Jimbo's Fish Shanty/SM | 17 | 14 | 16 | $17 |

245 Northern Ave. (adjacent to Boston Fish Pier), 542-5600
M – This fish house on the pier opposite Jimmy's Harborside has the same owner, but no view; prices, however, are lower and the big portions of "good fresh fish" attract families; kids like the working train set, and everyone likes the "good value" and "fast" service, though some think it "should be better"

Boston | F | D | S | C |

Jimmy Mac's | 21 | 10 | 13 | $14 |
300 Beacon St. (Eustis St.), Somerville, 547-1770
M – At this new barbecue in Somerville, families go for the moderately priced ribs, dry-rub barbecue and other Southern dishes, though not for the room or the "surly" service.

Jimmy's Harborside/M | 18 | 17 | 17 | $27 |
242 Northern Ave. (adjacent to Boston Fish Pier), 423-1000
M – Many of our Survey participants think the factory-like setting of this fish house with a harbor view has worn out its welcome, and are annoyed at the preferential treatment "pols" receive; nonetheless, it's unquestionably a Boston landmark and has food good enough to keep it crowded with tourists as well as natives taking out-of-towners.

Joe's American Bar & Grill/LSM | 15 | 16 | 15 | $19 |
279 Dartmouth St. (bet. Newbury St. & Commonwealth Ave.), 536-4200
M – A popular Back Bay bar and "trendy pick-up" spot where an under-30 crowd lines up for "surprisingly good" burgers and chowder at sensible prices; while better than you might expect, many still think it's best left to date-seekers.

Joe Tecce's/LSM | 17 | 15 | 16 | $24 |
61 N. Washington St. (Cooper St.), 742-6210
M – The definition of North End Italian, with "gaudy" decor and "red sauce to the max", this spot gets mixed reviews; a few think it's "unbeatable", but others say it's "embarrassing" and has slow service; convenience to Boston Garden is a plus.

Johnny D's | 15 | 15 | 15 | $16 |
17 Holland St. (Davis Sq.), Somerville, 776-2004
U – This crowded Somerville bar serves acceptable Eclectic food at low prices, but the food "takes second place to the music every time"; rhythm and blues, country and western and jazz bands make this a "great place for a lively evening."

Jonah's/LSM | 15 | 18 | 16 | $25 |
Hyatt Regency Hotel, 575 Memorial Dr. (bet. Mass. Ave. & B.U. Bridges), Cambridge, 492-1234
U – The "decent" though uninspired American-Continental food is pricey at this "pretty" Cambridge Hyatt Regency dining room, but people don't seem to mind – they report liking the "relaxing brunch", health-conscious dishes and Friday seafood buffet; perhaps this restaurant's name is prophetic.

Boston | F | D | S | C |

Joseph's Aquarium/SM | 17 | 16 | 16 | $24 |
101 Atlantic Ave. (Richmond St.), 523-4000
M – Diners are divided about this seafood place near Faneuil Hall and the waterfront; while many enjoy the "quiet atmosphere" and praise the reasonably priced lobster specials, others question the freshness of the fish and counsel, "avoid."

Joyce Chen/LSM | 17 | 15 | 16 | $19 |
115 Stuart St. (Tremont St.), 720-1331
390 Rindge Ave. (near Alewife MBTA station), Cambridge, 492-7373
M – Boston's most famous Chinese has two locations, the big "factory" near Fresh Pond in Cambridge and a trimly modern one in the Theater District; most diners consider them standbys and like the convenience of the Downtown branch, but dissenters feel it's "living off its name."

JULIEN/M | 26 | 26 | 25 | $47 |
Hotel Meridien, 250 Franklin St. (Pearl St.), 451-1900
U – This French Nouvelle strikes the great majority as "total class" and the "most elegant in Boston"; agreeing that it's "impressive", our respondents hail the room with its soaring ceiling; the speedy and well-priced business lunches are popular, and at night it's an "excellent choice for a special celebration" that's "worth the money"; the adjoining bar, with 1920s murals and piano music, is often called the "best" in town.

Karoun | 18 | 13 | 17 | $22 |
261 Walnut St. (Washington St.), Newtonville, 964-3400
M – With belly dancing on weekends, this Newtonville Armenian gets points just for novelty; those who go like the "friendly" service and consider the grilled lamb and other kebabs "reliable"; a few complain of paying too much for "nothing special."

Kebab-N-Kurry/SM | 18 | 8 | 14 | $17 |
30 Massachusetts Ave. (bet. Beacon & Marlboro Sts.), 536-9835
M – Opinion is sharply divided on this "crowded" Indian – it's either "delicious" or "the worst", with either "extremely slow" or "polite and efficient" service; students like the moderate prices.

Ken's Steak House | 18 | 14 | 18 | $24 |
95 Worcester Rd. (Rte. 9), Framingham, 508-235-5414
M – "Dependable" or "mediocre", this "basic steak house" has become a Framingham standby; "depressingly archaic" surroundings and a staff that's "a bit self-important" both draw criticism, however.

Boston | F | D | S | C |

King & I/SM | 20 | 12 | 18 | $17 |
145 Charles St. (near Charles Circle), 227-3320
259 Newbury St. (Fairfield St.), 437-9611
U – These two family-run Thais draw crowds for curries and pad thais in simple surroundings, with prices to match; however, what keeps them so popular are the "friendly folk" who make people regard these as the "most charming" Thais in Boston; lunch is recommended.

Kowloon | 18 | 18 | 17 | $18 |
948 Broadway (Main St.), Saugus, 233-0077
M – "Big and noisy", this "better-than-average" but somewhat weary Chinese fully qualifies as a "factory" as well as an "institution"; surveyors recommend "sitting near the volcano mural to fully enjoy the high camp experience" and ordering from the "tasty Thai menu"; the new comedy club also gets a thumbs-up.

Kyoto Japanese Steak House/SM | 18 | 14 | 18 | $23 |
201 Stuart St. (across from Howard Johnson's Hotel), 542-1166
M – There's "a lot of flourish, but little authenticity" at this knife-show Japanese grill in the Theater District; the food's not much better than "decent" and the atmosphere's "greasy and smoke-filled", but many – especially the kids – find this place a once-a-year dose of "fun."

La Espanola* | 21 | 11 | 18 | $15 |
405 Centre St. (near S. Huntington Ave.), Jamaica Plain, 524-9450
U – For "great Cuban country cooking" (never mind the "awful decor and surroundings"), this garlic-intensive Jamaica Plain storefront more than satisfies, especially when one gets the modest bill.

La Groceria Ristorante Italiano/SM | 19 | 16 | 17 | $22 |
853 Main St. (Bishop Allen Dr.), Cambridge, 497-4214
M – A "lively", "casual" neighborhood spot for "reliable" Italian food; although a few say that it has "gone downhill in the last year"; the clear majority goes for its "straightforward and well-executed" menu and crowded-but-fun atmosphere; "an Italian family's family restaurant"; N.B. there may be a wait.

Boston | F | D | S | C |

Landing, The | 13 | 15 | 14 | $19 |
81 Front St. (State St.), Marblehead, 631-1878
U – The redeeming factor of this harbor-view fish shack is "the outside porch overlooking the harbor"; for most of our surveyors the "noisy and unattractive" surroundings, unexciting "bar food" and "waitresses who would rather be sailing" add up to a "singles bar" where you'd best "bring your own food."

La Rivage* | 24 | 23 | 24 | $36 |
7 Water St. (Padanaram Bridge), Dartmouth, 508-999-4505
U – Woefully underrecognized is this "outstanding French" restaurant in the Buzzard's Bay area; though not cheap, it's beginning to get a reputation as one of "the best in the area", with "excellent" food and "nice people" running the show.

Las Brisas/SM | 13 | 15 | 15 | $18 |
70 E. India Row (Atlantic Ave.), 720-1820
M – Opinions are wildly divergent on this waterfront Mexican restaurant, from "prefab chain-food" to "Boston's best Mexican"; happy hours (with free hors d'oeuvre), margaritas and dancing to live music Thursday-Sunday win many fans, and the buffet gets high marks with the kiddies, but by and large, this "basic Mexican" is "nothing special."

Last Hurrah/LSM | 14 | 14 | 14 | $20 |
Omni Parker House, 60 School St. (Tremont St.), 227-8600
M – The "comfortable", nostalgic atmosphere and the "great eavesdropping" (on lawyers and politicians) are more fondly regarded than the "overpriced, boring Yankee cuisine", but if you stick to the standards – "wonderful, creamy clam chowder", hamburgers and those great Parker House rolls – you'll get a decent meal in a "fun place."

La Summa | 20 | 13 | 19 | $23 |
30 Fleet St. (North & Hanover Sts. at Moon St.), 523-9503
M – Another of "the North End's hidden gems", this "consistently enjoyable" Italian standby is run by a "nice family" who see to it that "no one rushes you here"; naysayers say it's slipping a bit.

La Trattoria/LSM | 18 | 14 | 16 | $21 |
288 Cambridge St. (near Mass General), 227-0211
M – Though a "good neighborhood Italian" for Beacon Hill, this would fare poorly in the North End, say unimpressed non-locals; the "basic" menu is "good, but nothing exceptional" and the room is "too little, too dark and too smoky" to pick up any slack.

Boston | F | D | S | C |

Le Bellecoeur | 19 | 17 | 18 | $30 |

10 Muzzey St. (near Massachusetts Ave.), Lexington, 861-9400

M – The "good but not outstanding" food doesn't quite make up for the pomposity of this Classic French; many surveyors would like more generosity in both portions and management, as well as "some creativity"; while an evening here can be "pleasant", it's rarely special.

LE BOCAGE/M | 24 | 19 | 22 | $38 |

72 Bigelow Ave. (off Mt. Auburn St.), Watertown, 923-1210

M – "They try and most often succeed" at this Watertown storefront French with "well-prepared, traditional, fresh food" and an "attentive, knowledgeable staff"; however, there is the occasional "disappointed" respondent who finds the ambiance "self-conscious", the prix-fixe menu "outdated" and the prices unwarranted.

LEGAL SEA FOODS/SM | 23 | 15 | 17 | $24 |

Park Plaza Hotel, 35 Columbus Ave. (Park Sq.), 426-4444
100 Huntington Ave. (Copley Pl., bet. Dartmouth & Exeter Sts.), 266-7775
5 Cambridge Center (Kendall Sq.), Cambridge, 864-3400
43 Boylston St. (bet. Hammond St. & Hammond Pond Pkwy.), Chestnut Hill, 277-7300
Burlington Mall, 1131 Middlesex Tpke. (Rte. 128), Burlington, 270-9700
1 Exchange Place (across from The Centrum), Worcester, 792-1600
1400 Worcester Rd. (across from Shoppers World), Natick, 508-820-1115

M – Once again, this seafood chain drew the most comment of any restaurant in the Survey, so it's not surprising that so many complain of "annoyingly overcrowded" and clamorous conditions at its many branches; as for the food, the majority still find it "consistently excellent", "always fresh" and "perfectly prepared"; locals recommend Kendall Square as the best (and calmest) overall; the new Copley Square branch is "surprisingly pretty."

Le Grande Cafe | 17 | 14 | 11 | $15 |

651 Boylston St. (bet. Dartmouth & Newbury Sts.), 437-6400
Mall at Chestnut Hill, Rte. 9 (bet. Hammond Pond Pkwy. & Langley Rd.), Chestnut Hill, 244-3100

M – Most surveyors "can take or leave" this Back Bay purveyor of Continental fast food and its new sibling in Chestnut Hill; although many find the sandwiches "tasty" and the rest of the menu "ok", "serious attitude problems" among the wait staff and questions about the prices spoil the fun.

Boston | F | D | S | C |

L'ESPALIER/M | 27 | 26 | 25 | $56 |
30 Gloucester St. (bet. Newbury St. & Commonwealth Ave.), 262-3023
M – *For a restaurant with ratings this spectacular, this Back Bay Classic French gets surprisingly mixed reviews from our surveyors; few disagree that "when money is no object, it's heaven", with the "exquisite", "artfully presented" food of Frank McClelland, a "lovely setting" and "very formal" service – in short, the "fanciest in Boston"; however, "haughty" waiters can make you feel "like the village idiot", and though it's arguably "the best in Boston", for many it's "too expensive for what you get."*

Little Osaka/SM | 20 | 16 | 19 | $19 |
465 Concord Ave. (near Fresh Pond Pkwy.), Cambridge, 491-6600
U – *A "diamond in the rough" to many Japanese food fans, this "forgotten little place" in Fresh Pond is "homey, cozy and a good value"; the "reliable home cooking" is "good but not outstanding", and though the reception can sometimes be a trifle "cool", that somehow only adds to the authentic feel.*

Loading Zone | 16 | 23 | 16 | $20 |
150 Kneeland St. (Lincoln St.), 695-0087
M – *"A nice place to visit" though many people disagree about the food, this "fun, trendy spot" Downtown is hands down "one of the most original ideas" to hit Boston, with its "post-industrial, post-nuclear environment" and tabletops that are also artworks; the BBQ can be either "magical" or "terrible" depending on the night, but one thing that doesn't change is the "friendly but spacey" service.*

LOCKE-OBER CAFE/SM | 21 | 22 | 22 | $39 |
3 Winter Place (bet. Tremont & Washington Sts.), 542-1340
M – *This "last bastion of Brahmin Boston" is simply "on a different level" from every other restaurant in town, for better or worse; if your tastes run to "utterly dependable" American food, "gentlemanly quarters" heavy on the "dark wood" and "waiters who are waiters, not friends", you'll find it "magically charming"; the uncharmed object to the "boring New England cuisine", "tired and grumpy" staff and an "atmosphere of testosterone."*

Los Andes* | 13 | 13 | 10 | $26 |
349 Centre St. (Westerly St.), Jamaica Plain, 524-9238
U – *This South American is one of the few of its genre in the Boston area, and is regarded by the few who know it as nice to have around its Jamaica Plain neighborhood, but nonetheless "overrated and overpriced."*

Boston | F | D | S | C |

L'Osteria/S | 21 | 12 | 18 | $22 |
109 Salem St. (Parmenter St.), 723-7847
U – Most are "never disappointed" by this "excellent Italian hole-in-the-wall" that's a long-time "North End favorite"; when the prices are this right for "superior" food, it's immaterial that the room is "teeny" and "messy", service is genial but sometimes careless and "lines on weekends terribly long."

Lucia's Ristorante/LSM | 19 | 16 | 17 | $25 |
415 Hanover St. (Harris St.), 367-2353
53 Mt. Vernon St. (Church St.), Winchester, 729-4585
M – Perhaps too well-known as the site of "Boston's most garish Italian decor" ("you don't know whether to laugh or to cry"), but if you choose carefully and stick to chicken and veal dishes, you can do fine at this North Ender and its Winchester sibling; the service is almost as kitschy as the mock-Sistine Chapel ceiling.

Lucky Garden/SM | 17 | 8 | 15 | $15 |
282 Concord Ave. (near Huron Ave.), Cambridge, 354-9514
M – "Yucky Garden" is probably more like it, say surveyors of this "once decent" but now "slightly greasy" Harvard Square Chinese; a sizable minority deems it "a delightful little nook", "friendly", "dependable, cheap and good enough."

Lyceum Bar & Grill | 18 | 20 | 18 | $22 |
43 Church St. (Washington St.), Salem, 508-745-7665
M – This "quaint" Salem grill has "recovered nicely under new ownership"; "pretty, but not intimate", its piano music and "passable" (though rapidly improving) food appeals to an older crowd.

Magic Pan/SM | 12 | 13 | 13 | $16 |
47 Newbury St. (Berkeley St.), 267-9315
Faneuil Hall Marketplace (Quincy Mkt. Bldg.), 523-6103
South Shore Plaza, 250 Granite St. (off Rte. 128), Braintree, 848-4220
Burlington Mall, 1131 Middlesex Tpke. (Rte. 128), Burlington, 272-3660
M – They're "quick", "conveniently located" and "reasonably priced", but most feel that at the branches of this "bogus" crepe chain, the "meals are flat" in more ways than one; expect a "good variety" of "average at best" selections served by "college student waiters" – but not bad for a light meal.

Boston

| | F | D | S | C |

MAISON ROBERT/M | 23 | 22 | 22 | $40 |
45 School St. (bet. Tremont & Washington Sts.), 227-3370
M – With "gracious dining in a historic setting" in the Old City Hall, this Classic French delivers the goods, even if its "staid and respectable" air doesn't appeal to all; the food is "wonderful" to some, though to others it "could be more creative"; similar mixed reactions greet the service and decor, which elicit responses from "top-notch" to "atrocious, '70s-style"; most raters agree, however, that it's at its best at lunch in the cafe.

Mamma Maria/SM | 22 | 21 | 22 | $35 |
3 North Square (Little Prince St.), 523-0077
U – This "top-notch North End eatery" "breaks all the rules – it uses 'mamma' and it's got good food!"; it's a "cozy getaway" with "outstanding" Nuova Cucina cooking that puts it "among the best Italians in the area", though not necessarily the most authentic; rising prices displease a few, who also would welcome a bit more consistency, but the majority considers it "romantic and delicious."

Marino's | – | – | – | M |
2465 Massachusetts Ave. (bet. Porter Sq. & Washburn St.), Cambridge, 868-5454
This very ambitious new Cambridge Italian prides itself on cooking everything from scratch, and even of growing much of its produce; the culinary results are of high quality, but strike some as bland; most like the cleanly-designed room with its open kitchen, but aren't so sure about service that can be a little overfamiliar.

Mary Chung/SMX | 21 | 8 | 14 | $15 |
447 Massachusetts Ave. (2 blocks from Central Sq.), Cambridge, 864-1991
U – An "MIT tradition" for its "great dim sum and dun-dun noodles", this "very Cambridge" Chinese is "always satisfying"; while it exerts a certain funky charm, even loyalists concede it "needs a degreasing."

Masada/LSM | 13 | 10 | 13 | $14 |
1665 Beacon St. (Winthrop Rd.), Brookline, 277-3433
M – Here's a "cheap, safe bet" for Israeli food that's healthy if bland; "good if you're with vegetarian friends", this Brookliner can't be counted on for more than an "adequate" meal, although those who like Middle Eastern might become fans.

Boston | F | D | S | C |

Mass Bay Company/SM | 16 | 14 | 16 | $25 |
Sheraton Boston Hotel, 39 Dalton St. (bet. Boylston St. & Huntington Ave.), 236-8787
M – Drooping ratings suggest that this Sheraton seafooder with a natty nautical setting has lost its way; once fashionable, it has "become too expensive" and the food has reportedly turned "mundane"; while you can still "make a meal out of the bread and chowder", nothing about this place inspires our surveyors.

Massimino's* | 22 | 20 | 21 | $17 |
207 Endicott St. (bet. N. Washington & Thatcher Sts.), 523-5959
U – For a "very inexpensive taste of the North End", our voters tout this Italian for its "very fresh" food, "good service" and "loads of charm"; it's a "personal, individual, old-style place" that's getting more crowded all the time.

Mateo's* | 19 | 11 | 17 | $18 |
351 Hanover St. (bet. Little Prince & Fleet Sts.), 523-9265
U – "A hidden Italian spot" in the North End that serves "great, original food" in a "cozy, not posh" storefront; with just one waiter, patience becomes a virtue, but the reward comes when you're served.

Matsu-ya/SM | 19 | 13 | 16 | $18 |
1790 Massachusetts Ave. (bet. Arlington & Lancaster Sts.), Cambridge, 491-5091
M – A "very reasonable" and satisfying, if unexceptional, Japanese-Korean near Porter Square, this "modestly decorated" spot "deserves more attention"; though there are dissenters who point to "slow, surly service" and insist the "food has gone downhill", the noodle soups and mouth-searing kim chee both have their champions.

Mattapoisett Inn | 19 | 19 | 20 | $28 |
13 Water St. (across from Mattapoisett Harbor), Mattapoisett, 508-758-4922
U – A "rustic", "Yankee-type setting" yields "good basic dining" at this "lovely old inn"; the Eclectic regional cooking comes with few surprises, but it doesn't interfere with one's enjoyment of the setting.

Medieval Manor | 9 | 17 | 15 | $26 |
246 E. Berkeley St. (Albany St.), 423-4900
U – This gimmicky Middle Ages theme restaurant where servers are actors and diners eat with their hands is "infantile beyond words" – though it can be fun if you "go with a group"; still, for most of our respondents, the air of "enforced merriment" "and undistinguished fare" mean that "once is enough."

Boston

| F | D | S | C |

Mexican Cuisine/SM | 22 | 9 | 15 | $18 |
1682 Massachusetts Ave. (bet. Harvard & Porter Sqs.), Cambridge, 661-1634
U – A "dive" that's "grungy but wonderful", with "fresh", "relatively cheap" and "reasonably authentic" Mexican dishes that some deem "Boston's best"; though inevitably crowded and noisy – some find the locals milling about the bar positively scary – "the food makes it easy to forgive" any shortcomings.

Michael's Waterfront/SM | 17 | 18 | 18 | $27 |
85 Atlantic Ave. (on the Waterfront), 367-6425
M – With "a wine list so unbelievable you almost overlook the satisfactory food", this harborside steak house and seafoodery has found a following; the "homey feeling" of the library-like room works to its advantage, as does the view.

MICHELA'S | 24 | 21 | 21 | $36 |
1 Athenaeum St. (bet. 1st & 2nd Sts.), Cambridge, 225-3366
M – This Northern Italian trendsetter, led by the stylish Michela Larson, has gone "up and down" since chef Todd English left, but "when it's hot it's hot" – and since chef Jody Adams, formerly of Hamersley's, moved to Cambridge, it's hot again; the "spartan" decor and noise bother some, and so do the prices in the dining room, but many reviewers call its atrium cafe "one of the best deals in the city", and everyone swoons over the "great bread."

Milk Street Cafe/MX | 18 | 9 | 12 | $11 |
50 Milk St. (Devonshire St.), 542-2433, 542-FOOD
350 Longwood Ave. (Brookline Ave.), 739-2233
101 Main St. (near the foot of Longfellow Bridge), Cambridge, 491-8287
M – Open only for breakfast and lunch, these "heavy on the sprouts" kosher dairy spots win favor for their "wholesome, healthy" choices and "reasonable prices", but our surveyors look askance at the "disorganized service" and often "bland" tastes.

Mill Falls/M | 19 | 21 | 20 | $34 |
383 Elliot St. (Chestnut St.), Newton Upper Falls, 244-3080
M – A favorite of businesspeople and "the blue-rinse set", this "romantic" suburban Contemporary American overlooking the Charles River Upper Falls probably merits higher food ratings since the arrival of chef Walter Zuromski, who has added new life to the kitchen; the staff is polished but a bit overbearing and the room itself, while "lovely", can come off as "prissy."

Boston | **F** | **D** | **S** | **C** |

Ming Garden/LSM | 16 | 12 | 15 | $17 |
1262 Boylston St. (across from Star Market Shopping Ctr.),
Chestnut Hill, 232-4848
*M – There's not much enthusiasm for this suburban
"highway Chinese" known for its "really good buffet",
but also unfortunately for its "dismal" if somewhat
elaborate atmosphere, "throw-the-food-at-you-style"
service and a kitchen that has begun its journey to
"Grease City."*

MISTER LEUNG'S/LSM | 23 | 22 | 22 | $34 |
545 Boylston St. (bet. Clarendon & Dartmouth Sts.),
236-4040
*M – Copley Square's "snazzy Chinese place" has many
partisans, who adore its "tranquil setting", "artistic
presentations", "subtle flavors" and "impeccable service";
naysayers call the food "sanitized", the decor "fading"
(redecoration is in the works) and service "erratic", and
figure that for these prices you should get perfection.*

Miyako/SM | 22 | 14 | 22 | $19 |
468 Commonwealth Ave. (bet. Mass. Ave. &
Kenmore Sq.), 236-0222
*U – Especially welcome in its Kenmore Square
neighborhood is this "favorite sushi restaurant" (though
the other Japanese dishes aren't always as successful); if
it's atmosphere you seek, "there are better", but if
you're in the area there are far worse that cost more.*

Montien/SM | 19 | 15 | 18 | $19 |
63 Stuart St. (bet. Tremont & Washington Sts.), 338-5600
*U – This "nice surprise" of a Thai has become a pre-
theater favorite; surveyors pay no heed to the "1980
New York pretentious decor" and turn their attention to
the "yummy" pad thai; the "staff is friendly", too; not
the culinary experience of a lifetime, but very useful.*

Moon Villa/LSM | 14 | 7 | 12 | $14 |
19 Edinboro St. (bet. Essex & Kingston Sts.), 423-2061
*M – Its greatest virtues are that it's "open all night" and
the "price is right" – otherwise, there's little reason to
note this "unfashionable" Combat Zone Chinese
specializing in "decent" "everyday" food; even more
than a good cook, this place "needs a good cleaning."*

Boston | F | D | S | C |

MORTON'S OF CHICAGO/M | 24 | 17 | 21 | $37 |
1 Exeter Place (bet. Exeter & Dartmouth Sts.), 266-5858
U – "Leave your vegetarian friends at home" when you enter this ineffably "macho" Back Bay steak house; it bases its reputation on "lotsa meat" of very high quality, and many say it's got the "best steaks in Boston", though less carnivorous sorts proclaim it "big, beefy and boring"; watch out for "too many add-ons", or you'll find you could "eat twice elsewhere for less."

Mother Anna's | 21 | 16 | 18 | $24 |
211 Hanover St. (Cross St.), 523-8496
U – "Clearly above average", "easy and reliable", this North End Italian is a "jewel" for the area; seating is as "limited" as the portions are "gargantuan"; prices should probably be a bit lower and waiters a bit more attentive, but dependability always has its price.

Mr. Bartley's Burger Cottage/MX | 20 | 9 | 14 | $10 |
1246 Massachusetts Ave. (near Harvard Sq.), Cambridge, 354-6559
U – If these aren't the "best hamburgers in the universe", they're certainly the best around the city: this collegiate joint in Harvard Square looks like a salady fern bar, but "don't let the decor fool you" – it's grease heaven, with great onion rings, too, and "the price is right"; "there's no other place like it and if there is, I don't want to know about it."

Museum of Fine Arts Restaurant/S | 16 | 19 | 15 | $21 |
465 Huntington Ave. (Museum Rd. entrance), 267-9300 ext. 474
M – There are as many opinions on this museum rest stop, whose menu changes with new exhibitions, as there are opinions on modern art; for every respondent who loves the garden views and says it's "a pleasant place to take tourists" (or dates), another one terms it "uninspired"; "once an embarrassment, now pretty good", it's still not good enough to avoid the question, "they have fine art, why not fine food?"

Nadia's Eastern Star/LSMX | 17 | 8 | 16 | $15 |
280 Shawmut Ave. (bet. Tremont St. & Columbus Ave.), 338-8091
U – A "quirky, out-of-the-way place" serving "simple, honest" Lebanese food, this South End spot is a godsend "if you're on a really tight budget"; when you're filled with garlic chicken and "Mama's making stuffed grape leaves in the dining room", no one cares that it's a little "seedy."

Boston | **F** | **D** | **S** | **C** |

Nara Restaurant/M | 21 | 12 | 17 | $21 |
85 Wendell St. (Broad St.), 338-5935
U – "Hidden in an alley" is a "well-kept secret" that may be one of Boston's best sushi spots – though that's not to denigrate the rest of the Japanese-Korean menu; neither the ambiance nor the service is noticeable enough to interfere with the meal.

NAVONA | 23 | 25 | 22 | $32 |
415 Whiting St. (near Rte. 3), Hingham, 337-0757
M – With its "wonderful setting" in (of all things) a renovated former quarry building, this Italian-American with a French flair is often capable of culinary greatness; however, on the kitchen's rare off-day, the place can seem merely "pretentious"; many feel it's a contender for the title of "South Shore's best."

Neighborhood Restaurant/SMX | 20 | 13 | 16 | $13 |
25 Bow St. (Union Sq.), Somerville, 623-9710
U – "Paul Bunyan would be happy" with the enormous portions of simple, tasty food at this plain, family-run Portuguese restaurant; best known for its bountiful breakfasts and "brunch beyond belief", this place is underrated for dinner; "the new grape arbor with picnic tables is great."

New Bridge Cafe/SMX | 22 | 9 | 17 | $13 |
650 Washington Ave. (Woodlawn Ave.), Chelsea, 884-0134
M – One of "the last of the great values" is this Chelsea BBQ joint famous for its "steak tips nonpareil" and its ribs; however, you have to put up with a room that's "too small and has no windows", as well as noise, smoke and waits; "I always get indigestion, but always seem to return."

Newbury Steak House/LSM | 12 | 11 | 13 | $18 |
94 Massachusetts Ave. (bet. Newbury St. & Commonwealth Ave.), 536-0184
M – "How does it survive?"; this "relic" of a Back Bay steak house strikes most respondents as "pathetic", with "tough looks" from the wait staff and "tough tastes" on the plate, not to mention "cramped booths" and a "too-dark atmosphere"; the only explanation is that it's cheap, convenient, highly visible and evokes "memories of college."

Boston | F | D | S | C |

New House of Toy* | 20 | 10 | 15 | $17 |
16 Hudson St. (bet. Kneeland & Beech Sts.), 426-5587
U – "Great dim sum" in a spiffy, newly remodeled Chinatown location is the line on this newcomer; though more costly than the original House of Toy, and more crowded, most surveyors find the food "worth it."

New Korea/S | 21 | 8 | 19 | $17 |
1281 Cambridge St. (Prospect St.), Cambridge, 876-6182
U – For Korean in Cambridge, you can't do much better than this "ugly place" that nonetheless offers "creative food", "lovely people" and "most attentive service"; if you're new to the cuisine, you'd be wise to let the waitress order for you.

Newtowne Grille | 13 | 8 | 13 | $13 |
1945 Massachusetts Ave. (bet. Davenport & Allen Sts.), Cambridge, 661-0706
M – If a "cheap bowl of spaghetti" is all you're after, try this "honest" Porter Square "neighborhood joint" that's "a touch plastic, but cozy"; naysayers cite "the worst pizza in Boston", and pronounce it "just awful."

New Yorker Diner | 18 | 12 | 17 | $10 |
39 Mt. Auburn St. (Summer St.), Watertown, 924-9772
U – This suburbanite is exactly "what a diner should be – greasy"; long near the top of the list for the late-late crowd, it's got unobtrusive service and "great ham and eggs"; "nothing special", but "see you at 2 AM for dinner."

Nicole* | 23 | 20 | 21 | $23 |
54 Salem St. (bet. Cross & Parmenter Sts.), 742-6999
U – Rapidly developing a buzz among food cognoscenti is this newly discovered North End "secret" with "really wonderful" Italian food that tastes utterly "homemade"; in its "small but cozy" premises the "friendly, attentive service" can falter, but with the kitchen working this well and value high, who can complain?

Noble House | 19 | 17 | 18 | $19 |
1306 Beacon St. (Coolidge Corner), Brookline, 232-9580
M – On a good day, this "upscale, modern" spot may be "the best Chinese restaurant outside Chinatown", but it's not consistent; skeptics would like "a surer hand with the sauces", while fans praise the "tasteful decoration" and "high quality" fare; on the whole, "a cut above the usual."

Boston | F | D | S | C |

No Name/MX | 17 | 8 | 13 | $16 |
15½ Fish Pier (off Northern Ave.), 338-7539
M – "Still cheap, greasy and fun", this Waterfront seafoodery is a sort of litmus test – if you find charm in its mix of raffish surroundings, "rough service" ("the Saturday Night Live Greek diner crew doing seafood"), pervasive odor of fried fish, "unbearable" noise and low prices, you'll have a great time; otherwise, it'll be a "gross, dirty, smelly" experience that "abuses seafood and diners"; some feel getting a liquor license was a "major error."

OASIS CAFE | 23 | 18 | 20 | $16 |
176 Endicott St. (bet. N. Washington & Thatcher Sts.), 523-9274
U – Devotees go for the "great old-fashioned American food and Ella Fitzgerald on the jukebox" at this North Ender that, for once, isn't Italian; a few come away "disappointed", but most like the "good value", "huge portions" and casual atmosphere.

O'Fado* | 21 | 14 | 18 | $18 |
52 Walnut St. (near Central St.), Peabody, 508-531-7369
U – "One of the bright spots of the North Shore" makes a specialty of "home-style Portuguese" fare in heaping quantities "for few escudos"; everything else is less than memorable, but if you're looking for "something really different", this is a "nice surprise."

Oh Calcutta | 18 | 12 | 19 | $16 |
16 Irving St. (Rtes. 126 & 135), Framingham, 508-875-6212
U – Though there may be "better Indian food in town", this spot is undeniably "good for the suburbs", and an especially "good value" if you're willing to overlook a dowdy room.

OLIVES | 27 | 18 | 20 | $32 |
67 Main St. (Monument Ave.), Charlestown, 242-1999
M – The good news is that this foodie favorite in yuppie-invaded Charlestown is "the hottest spot in town", with "phenomenal" Northern Italian-Mediterranean cooking under the direction of Todd English, and "affordable, too"; the problem is, "they make it as difficult as possible to eat here" – it's cramped and "full of commotion", and the no-reservations policy for groups of fewer than 6 often results in long waits.

Boston | F | D | S | C |

On the Park/S | 21 | 16 | 19 | $22 |
315 Shawmut Ave. (Union Park), 426-0862
U – This "above average neighborhood restaurant" "works 9 out of 10 times" with its "creative, stylish, healthy" American menu; the funky but cutesy air isn't to everyone's taste ("if Pee Wee Herman owned a restaurant, he would decorate it like this"), nor do many care for the "tables on top of each other"; however, most feel "more of its kind are needed in Boston."

On the Square | 21 | 21 | 19 | $32 |
9 Galen St. (Main St., Watertown Sq.), Watertown, 923-1522
U – For a "Downtown-quality restaurant in the suburbs", many point to this Northern Italian "sleeper" that's "innovative and reasonable"; granted, the kitchen can make things "too complicated", but the room is "lovely" and "very relaxing", and the "good wine program" is "fairly priced."

Open Sesame/SM | 14 | 10 | 13 | $14 |
48 Boylston St. (High St.), Brookline, 277-9241
M – "Transcending this world does not necessarily result in good cooking or service" say critics of this Brookliner, one of "the only macrobiotics in town"; it offers "New Age tasteless" fare in a "back to the '60s" setting marked by "slow service"; still, its vociferous fans hail the "very good vegetarian food" as "the best in Beantown."

Ottavio's | 17 | 16 | 18 | $27 |
257 North St. (Lewis St.), 723-6060
M – To loyalists it's "a real find in the North End", but others consider this Italian too uneven to warrant an unqualified recommendation; the "stereotypical Italian decor" may be "romantic", but many question the "high prices", especially for specials.

Pagliuca's Restaurant*/M | 19 | 12 | 17 | $23 |
14 Parmenter St. (near Hanover St.), 367-1504
U – If all you're looking for is good food at fair prices, you're likely to find this prototypical North End Italian "heavy on the red sauce" a "treat"; service, though, is unreliable and for some the "noisy bar ruins the atmosphere."

Boston

| F | D | S | C |

Palmer's*
| 26 | 16 | 20 | $30 |

408 Humphrey St. (Greenwood St.), Swampscott, 596-1820

U – Many more people should know about this truly "excellent" North Shore Italian that's "one of the best on the water from Revere to Rockport"; about the only disparaging comments anyone can make is that the kitchen "stretches sometimes" and that it's "too fancy and overpriced" for unassuming Swampscott.

Paparazzi
| 19 | 19 | 17 | $23 |

271 Dartmouth St. (bet. Newbury & Boylston Sts.), 536-9200

Mall at Chestnut Hill, Rte. 9 (bet. Hammond Pond Pkwy. & Langley Rd.), Chestnut Hill, 527-6600

U – Most find that the "good but not memorable" Italian food with a California twist, snappy service and the "best people-watching in town" make the relatively new Back Bay location "an improvement" over its previous occupant, Dartmouth Street; however, if watching "yuppies on the prowl" doesn't sound like your idea of a good time, you may choose to pass; the Chestnut Hill branch is brand-new.

PARKER'S/SM
| 23 | 24 | 24 | $37 |

Omni Parker House, 60 School St. (Tremont St.), 227-8600, ext. 1600

U – This is a "real Old Boston" bastion of "hearty" fare, stately and "attentive" service and "unabashed elegance" – a "classic in every sense"; go for the unequivocally "civilized brunch" to see it at its best.

P.A. Seafood/S
| 18 | 9 | 16 | $22 |

345 Somerville St. (Union Sq.), Somerville, 776-1557

M – A "long-time favorite" of those who enjoy wolfing down their "Portuguese delights" and "reliably good seafood" amid "red bordello decor"; however, even those respondents who applaud the food and "good value" weigh the service and surroundings at this Somerville old-timer and suggest it's "time for a new beginning."

Pattaya/S
| 19 | 16 | 18 | $18 |

1032 Beacon St. (bet. St. Mary's & Carlton Sts.), Brookline, 566-3122

M – Neck-and-neck with the "the best Thai" in Brookline – which has quite a few good ones; the kitchen's at very least "decent" and usually much better than that, the staff dispenses lots of smiles and the weekend all-you-can-eat brunch is a hit.

Boston | F | D | S | C |

Peacock Restaurant | 20 | 15 | 19 | $26 |
5 Craigie Circle (bet. Concord Ave. & Brattle St.),
Cambridge, 661-4073
*M – "You either love this place or think it's a bore" –
and many do love "the best-kept secret of Harvard
Square" for its "better-than-average food", "relaxed
setting" and "attention to detail"; the unenchanted find
the Country French cookery "dull" and "sometimes
heavy", and the basement location "clammy."*

Peking Garden/SM | 16 | 14 | 15 | $17 |
27 Waltham St. (Mass. Ave., Lexington Ctr.), Lexington,
862-1051
*U – "It used to be that the food made up for the service,
but no more", say disaffected surveyors about this
declining suburban Szechuan; the brunch buffet
remains "popular" with families, but "too many kids
spoil adult dining."*

Pentimento/SMX | 17 | 14 | 13 | $13 |
344 Huron Ave. (bet. Fayerweather & Guerny Sts.),
Cambridge, 661-3878
*U – Despite "heavenly desserts" and "wholesome food",
this "very Cambridge" museum of "hippie nostalgia"
strikes many as a case of "wasted potential"; a "politically
correct" staff needn't provide "head-in-the-clouds service."*

Pho Pasteur* | 21 | 6 | 16 | $9 |
8 Kneeland St. (bet. Washington & Stuart Sts.), 451-0247
*U – The specialty of this "good Vietnamese" in the
Theater District is soup – take your choice between
"the best chicken soup in the world" or "beef broth
heaven"; before a show it'll save you time and money,
and if you eat fast enough you won't notice the room.*

Piccola Venezia/SMX | 18 | 9 | 15 | $14 |
63 Salem St. (bet. Cross & Parmenter Sts.), 523-9802
*U – "A tried and true North End delight" with a
"homey atmosphere", this Italian's kitchen delivers
"lots of chow" that's "reliable and filling", but "nothing
fancy"; "casual, loud" and tiny, you'd better "get there
early" if you want any elbow room.*

Boston | F | D | S | C |

PILLAR HOUSE/M | 21 | 23 | 22 | $30 |
26 Quinobequin Rd. (intersection of Rtes. 16 & 95/128), Newton Lower Falls, 969-6500
M – Your opinion of this "steady" traditional American in a comfortable old Colonial home will depend on your palate's sense of adventure – one person's "very solid" is another's "boring"; a "sure bet for a special evening" or "impressing clients", this popular spot is trying to shed its reputation as an "old folks' home", not entirely successfully; closed on weekends.

PLAZA DINING ROOM | 23 | 25 | 23 | $49 |
(aka Cafe Plaza)
Copley Plaza Hotel, 138 St. James St. (Dartmouth St. at Copley Sq.), 267-5300
M – Is one of Boston's most expensive spots "worth the coin"? – most respondents think so, citing the "Victorian splendor" of the turn-of-the-century room, the "excellent Continental food" and "exquisite service" that "makes the food even better"; a few, while conceding that it's "a great place to impress someone", consider the cost excessive.

PONTE VECCHIO | 25 | 21 | 22 | $33 |
435 Newbury St. (before Topsfield Fairgrounds), Danvers, 508-777-9188
U – This "Italian sleeper in a shopping strip" has "real charisma" as well as "fresh and fantastic fish" as part of its "truly fine" menu; though a few question the courtesy level of the staff, most think that overall it "rivals Boston's best."

Porterhouse Cafe | 20 | 9 | 16 | $18 |
2046 Massachusetts Ave. (Creighton St.), Cambridge, 354-9793
U – The "latest BBQ contender" rides into Cambridge with "cheap, plentiful" ribs that "would impress Calvin Trillin"; most find the "real spicy" fare to their liking; if the "basic", grungy "barroom setting" isn't going to win any design awards, "who needs decor with food this good?"

Ports* | 21 | 25 | 19 | $47 |
Vista Hilton, 70 Third Ave. (Toten Pond Rd.), Waltham, 290-5600
U – While many appreciate the "old-world courtliness" of this "very plush" room in the Vista International, it's often felt to be "too pricey for what it is"; still, "for those on expense accounts" its Continental and seafood choices have enough attractions to make this an impressive place to do business.

Boston | F | D | S | C |

Portugalia* | 17 | 19 | 20 | $19 |
723 Cambridge St. (Tremont St.), Cambridge, 354-9340
M – This "relatively undiscovered" Inman Square Portuguese is hard to get a handle on; while some have found it "excellent" and "very welcoming", others have encountered "disappointment"; ratings indicate fans are in the majority.

Pour House | 13 | 12 | 15 | $10 |
907 Boylston St. (bet. Hereford & Gloucester Sts.), 236-1767
U – A "nice, cheap Back Bay dump" that's "not bad for a bar, but not good for a restaurant", this is a "hangout sort of place" where you can get a burger and a beer for five bucks; it's "great food for when you're drunk", but sobriety brings down the cuisine ratings; "downstairs has a serious case of the musties."

Pushcart, The | 19 | 11 | 17 | $18 |
61 Endicott St. (Cross St.), 523-9616
U – Celtics fans have anointed this North Ender near Boston Garden as a pre-game must for massive portions of basic Italian food; as if you couldn't guess, it's "small, noisy and crowded" – not to mention "too dark" – but nonetheless fun; families get especially good treatment from the "understanding staff."

Rama Thai/SM | 19 | 14 | 17 | $15 |
(fka Siam Palace)
379 Cambridge St. (Harvard St.), Allston, 783-2434
M – Newly renamed and remodeled, the food at this Thai is catching up with its other ambitions; despite the redo, decor remains a matter of taste, but the arrival of the liquor license is a definite plus.

RARITIES/SM | 23 | 24 | 23 | $46 |
Charles Hotel, 1 Bennett St. (Eliot St.), Cambridge, 864-1200, ext. 1214
M – This "beautiful" Nouvelle American "just misses the top rank"; "sometimes precious, but mostly exquisite", there's always "something inspired" on its "creative menu", and the service and wine list both win high praise; what keeps it from greatness, our surveyors suspect, is a way of "trying too hard."

Boston | F | D | S | C |

Rebecca's/LSM | 20 | 15 | 16 | $21 |
21 Charles St. (bet. Chestnut & Branch Sts.), 742-9747
112 Newbury St. (near Clarendon St.), 267-1122
18 Tremont St. (near Government Ctr.), 227-0020
56 High St. (bet. Federal & Congress Sts.), 951-2422
290 Main St. (Kendall Sq.), Cambridge, 494-6688
65 JFK St. (Harvard Sq.), Cambridge, 661-8989
M – These yuppie gourmet delis – except for the highly-regarded Charles Street location, which is a proper restaurant – turn out food that's "uninspired", though often "very good"; the muffins and scones bring a booming breakfast trade, but the "too self-conscious", "too anxious" service doesn't please many; though "a little expensive", they're generally considered "good standbys."

Redbones/SX | 21 | 12 | 17 | $17 |
55 Chester St. (off Elm St., near Davis Sq.), Somerville, 628-2200
U – For "noisy Southern fun", few spots can compete with this rib joint that many feel to have "the best BBQ in Boston", "better than some in Texas"; the point here is not the "down and dirty" setting or the "help that ride Harley-Davidsons" – it's the "awesome" "redneck-type" ribs, as well as a mean pulled pork sandwich; expect a wait.

Red Lion | 16 | 17 | 18 | $22 |
71 S. Main St. (Elm St.), Cohasset, 383-1704
U – This Cohasset "tradition" may be "always fun", but "the witches of Eastwick must have put a spell on the food"; the American fare comes in "generous amounts", but it tends to be "ordinary" and won't do much to improve your opinion if the raffish charm of the tiny space doesn't work for you.

RISTORANTE TOSCANO/SM | 24 | 19 | 21 | $34 |
41 Charles St. (bet. Mt. Vernon & Chestnut Sts.), 723-4090
M – The "only authentic Northern Italian in Boston", this Beacon Hill class-act has become a "local favorite" with its "wonderful menu" and "wonderful flavors"; a small number find it "correct but rather boring", but they're outvoted by those who say it's "absolutely fabulous."

Rita's Place | 23 | 10 | 20 | $28 |
88 Winnisimmet St. (Williams St.), Chelsea, 884-9010
U – This Southern Italian is generally "stuffed to the gills" and so are the patrons, on the "loads of food" served up; if prices seem "a bit expensive for a dive", so what? – it's the sort of "fun dining" everybody "should do at least once."

Boston | F | D | S | C |

RITZ CAFE/LSM | 21 | 23 | 24 | $28 |
Ritz-Carlton Hotel, 15 Arlington St. (Newbury St.), 536-5700
U – "When in doubt, it's still one of the best" – that's the prevailing view of this room of "lovely, quiet elegance" that's nonetheless "less fussy, less expensive and more fun" than the upstairs dining room at this classic Back Bay hotel; good, casual meals, business breakfasts and smooth, professional service are specialties here.

RITZ DINING ROOM/SM | 23 | 27 | 26 | $46 |
Ritz-Carlton Hotel, 15 Arlington St. (Newbury St.), 536-5700
M – While "always impressive", this "oasis of tradition" with its gorgeous formal decor and "unexcelled service" has slipped a bit in the eyes of quite a few surveyors; despite high ratings, some consider the fare "very uneven", though sometimes memorable, and the prices stiff; however, the new menu, with its spa and low-fat items, is said to be a winner; loyalists contend that "class tells."

ROCCO'S/S | 19 | 24 | 19 | $29 |
5 S. Charles St. (Boylston St.), 723-6800
M – Roughly half our raters find the "imaginative, self-conscious" International home cooking of Danny Weisel at this Theater District spot "strangely wonderful", while the other half says it "tries too hard"; all the rage last year, its "dramatic space" that resembles "an expensively appointed warehouse" still has lots of fans, though to the trend-resistant it's simply "too weird" and "quirky."

Roka/S | 23 | 19 | 19 | $23 |
1001 Mass. Ave. (bet. Harvard & Central Sqs.), Cambridge, 661-0344
U – Since reopening after a fire, "the food has vastly improved" at this "pleasant", "dependable" Cambridge Japanese; critics are of two minds toward the "ultra-moody" setting, but "sublime" sushi and "excellent, fresh Japanese dishes" win them over.

Rosalie's | 20 | 20 | 19 | $28 |
18 Sewall St. (bet. School & Elm Sts.), Marblehead, 631-5353
29 Hudson Rd. (Concord Rd.), Sudbury, 508-443-4300
M – Some say Rosalie was "coasting on her reputation" even before her local Italian-American institution appeared in a VISA commercial; but even if "it's not like it used to be", the "homey, comfortable atmosphere" and solid cooking still work for most people; the Sudbury location is new.

Boston | F | D | S | C |

ROWES WHARF RESTAURANT & CAFE
| 20 | 25 | 22 | $41 |

Boston Harbor Hotel, 70 Rowes Wharf (on Atlantic Ave.), 439-3995

M – If you're partial to its "masculine decor" and "marvelous view", you'll probably "love it here"; the regional New England menu, while often excellent thanks to the efforts of emerging star chef Daniel Bruce, "isn't always up to the rest of the place", and that includes the "pampering", though mildly "condescending", service.

Rubin's/SMX
| 19 | 8 | 15 | $14 |

500 Harvard St. (near Commonwealth Ave.), Brookline, 566-8761

U – Almost everyone finds Brookline's "imitation New York deli" "passable", but it's clearly "not up to NY standards"; "noise at all times" and help that defines "chutzpah" both show it's got parts of the act down, but the "bland corned beef" gives the game away; "it's hit-or-miss, but it's just about all we've got."

Rudy's Cafe/LSMX
| 18 | 12 | 15 | $13 |

248 Holland St. (near Davis Sq.), Somerville, 623-9201

M – This Somerville Mexican "used to be better", but to many surveyors "it has gone downhill since expansion"; nonetheless, many find it a valuable source of "good cheap eats" that "even Californians like"; just expect the usual threesome of youth, noise and crowding; there's takeout if you lack patience.

Sablone's Veal 'n Vintage/M
| 22 | 13 | 18 | $24 |

107A Porter St. (exit at local traffic ramp en route to Logan Airport), East Boston, 567-8140

U – The "clown motif's a bit much", but there's no clowning about the "best veal around" at this "friendly, consistent" Italian near Logan; the service gets mixed reviews, but pretty much everyone's agreed that, even at the price, this place is the veal thing.

Sabra
| 12 | 8 | 12 | $16 |

45 Union St. (Langley Rd.), Newton, 527-5641

U – Sure, it's "cheap and quick", but this suburban Israeli's dishes are often "poorly executed" and "everything tastes similar"; the "excellent salads" offer "good, simple value", but despite "anxious to please owners", "there are better places for this kind of food."

Boston | F | D | S | C |

Sakura-bana/SM | 22 | 15 | 19 | $20 |
57 Broad St. (Milk St.), 542-4311
U – A combination of "homey Japanese food" and a "warm and gentle staff" make this "neighborhood restaurant" in the Financial District "one of Boston's great little spots"; two tips: don't expect much atmosphere, and "go early for lunch."

Sally Ling's/SM | 20 | 19 | 19 | $27 |
10 Langley Rd. (Centre St.), Newton Center, 332-3600
Hyatt Regency Hotel, 575 Memorial Dr. (Amesberry St.), Cambridge, 868-1818
M – Lower ratings suggest that at these "upscale Chinese" "the care and concern seem to be disappearing"; while many voters still find them "classy", a growing group bemoans the "watered-down" cooking, "desultory" service and "high cost/quality ratio"; at least the Cambridge version's "breathtaking views" haven't changed.

Salty Dog/SM | 15 | 11 | 13 | $16 |
Faneuil Hall Marketplace (Center Bldg.), 742-2095
U – "If you're starving at Quincy Market", you'll find the seafood specialties here "fair fare", though if you expect very much you're in for "a disappointment"; the service is almost as perfunctory as the surroundings, but for the quality, the "prices are decent."

Sami's 24 Hours | 18 | 6 | 18 | $9 |
299 Longwood Ave. (Brookline Ave. & Ave. Louis Pasteur), 232-7175
U– Dependable, ultra-cheap and always open, "the saving grace of the Longwood medical area" dishes up Middle Eastern and Mexican fast food that's perfect for a "post-drinking, pre-hangover snack"; "you can't beat the prices or the hours", and a lot of people "love the guys" who run the place.

S & S Restaurant/LSMX | 18 | 13 | 16 | $13 |
1334 Cambridge St. (Inman Sq.), Cambridge, 354-0777
M – The vote is split between those who call this Inman Square institution "just a diner, but one of the best", and those who call its Jewish food "plastic"; if it's "not what it was", it's still "great for Sunday brunch" and "before or after Celtics games."

| **Boston** | **F** | **D** | **S** | **C** |

Santarpio's Pizza/SMX | 22 | 8 | 13 | $12 |

111 Chelsea St. (Porter St., local traffic ramp en route to Logan Airport), East Boston, 567-9468
U – The word here is pizza, period – to many it's "Boston's best", worth braving the schlep to East Boston, "tough waitresses" and "horrendous atmosphere"; the best advice is "get the garlic pizza and don't talk to anyone for a month."

SAPORITO | 27 | 16 | 23 | $31 |

11 Rockland Circle (1 block from Nantucket Ave.), Hull, 925-3023
U – It's "an adventure to find, but worth the search", our reviewers say of this "immediately likable" South Shore Northern Italian that's "smart, sassy" and "imaginative", with "lots of garlic"; though a few say the setting's not up to the food, getting a reservation remains very tough work – but worth the effort, because the "terrific" food and pleasant owners make it "a great find."

Saraceno's* | 21 | 18 | 21 | $26 |

286 Hanover St. (bet. Cross & Richmond Sts.), 227-5353
U – For "honest Sicilian-type food" in the North End, this little-known spot has a coterie of passionate fans; despite trite "murals and bad guitar serenades" – or perhaps because of them – the place has a "personal" feel that just makes the "wonderful food" even better.

Sawasdee/SM | 22 | 18 | 20 | $19 |

320 Washington St. (1 block from Harvard St.), Brookline Village, 566-0720
U – This "fresh-tasting Thai" is "possibly the best" in the area – the menu's "imaginative" and the dishes "show extra care in preparation"; decor and staff are both personable, and the only quibble anyone can muster is that it's sometimes "too noisy."

Schifino | 20 | 19 | 20 | $28 |

21 Broad St. (bet. State & Milk Sts.), 523-0590
M – An "ambitious menu, splendidly executed" draws fans of this "high-class Italian" Downtown yearling – "let's keep it a secret", they beg; but despite the "genuinely fine service", some "can't understand all the fuss" over a "pretty mediocre" "overachiever"; it's possible the yea-sayers are simply grateful for any "interesting food" in the area.

Boston | F | D | S | C |

Schroeder's | 16 | 16 | 17 | $24 |
8 High St. (Summer St.), 426-1234
M – "What's more tired – the decor or the help?" asks a representative surveyor of this Downtown "institution" with "old-world food and old-world service, but new-world prices"; while some grant that it's a "decent standby" for a business lunch, the "less than ordinary" fare and "crude service" leave many cold.

Scullers Grille/SM | 18 | 20 | 18 | $27 |
Guest Quarters Suites Hotel, 400 Soldiers Field Rd. (River St.), Allston, 783-0090
M – The good news is that this hotel grill is "a great place to hear jazz and watch the Charles", the bad news is that the "food looks great but tastes fair"; critics say the "uninspiring" fare comes in "too-large portions."

Seaside Restaurant/SM | 15 | 13 | 14 | $19 |
Faneuil Hall Marketplace (South Market Bldg.), 742-8728
U – "Very ordinary", "like most places at Faneuil Hall", this "dating bar" can be "fun for lunch" if you keep your expectations low; despite a reputation for seafood, the chicken salad is the best thing on the menu.

SEASONS/SM | 26 | 25 | 26 | $46 |
Bostonian Hotel, 9 Blackstone St. N. (bet. North & Blackstone Sts.), 523-3600
U – This finishing school for great Boston chefs – Jasper White, Lydia Shire, Bill Poirer and now the very talented Tony Ambrose – remains "consistently better than others in its price category"; though a few voters detect "signs of fatigue", the great majority contends that the mix of "inventive", "very, very rich" food, "great surroundings", "super wine list" and "pampering service" add up to dining that "doesn't get any better"; a major redo should raise the decor ratings even higher when it's finished.

Seoul House*/SM | 19 | 10 | 17 | $16 |
57 Union St. (across from Newton Ctr. MBTA stop), Newton Center, 244-6438
U – Despite slipping food ratings, this is "probably the best Korean food in Boston, which isn't saying much"; tiny and cramped, it's personable and "dependable", with a BYO policy that keeps prices down.

Boston | F | D | S | C |

Serendipity III/SM | 15 | 17 | 14 | $16 |
Faneuil Hall Marketplace (South Market Bldg.), 523-2339
U – With its tourist-friendly location and ice cream-intensive bill of fare, this is a kids' must; look for the foot-long hot dogs and the incomparable frozen hot chocolate, but don't be surprised if service is "sloppy" and the noise level is ear-splitting.

798 MAIN | 25 | 19 | 22 | $35 |
(fka Panache)
798 Main St. (Windsor St.), Cambridge, 876-8444
M – Since Bruce Frankel returned to his old stand and made extensive changes (including the name), opinion has been divided regarding this Nouvelle American with a regional twist; happily, for every critic who feels Frankel "has made a mistake", there are several more who like "the lowered prices and pretensions"; noise and "decor a la fishbowl" are recognized problems, but the "carefully prepared", if "a little uneven", food is usually "truly good."

Sevens, The | 12 | 14 | 13 | $11 |
77 Charles St. (bet. Beacon & Cambridge Sts.), 523-9074
U – A "great tavern to hang out in", say locals who call this Beacon Hill neighborhooder "the real Cheers", where "Beacon Hill ladies as well as bikers" and "the J. Crew crowd come to forget their troubles"; food's not the point here, but the French dip sandwich is worth a try.

Sfuzzi | 19 | 20 | 17 | $27 |
Atrium Mall, 300 Boylston St. (Heath St.), Chestnut Hill, 965-7707
M – While many find the local branch of this trendy Northern Italian chain "sfun!", with a "sfabulous look and sfantastic food", a number of others caution that "the food sftinks"; most find that the kitchen has "great potential", but doesn't quite cut it; the "large, bawdy crowd" and piped-in MTV are "irritating" if you're not in the mood.

Shalimar of India/S | 20 | 13 | 16 | $17 |
546 Massachusetts Ave. (Central Sq.), Cambridge, 547-9280
U – Its "rich and complicated tastes" make this Central Square Indian "a favorite", even though it can be "uneven"; the "housekeeping needs improving" and service is perfunctory; "ask for the food spicy" and you won't be disappointed.

Boston | F | D | S | C |

SHERBORN INN | 20 | 25 | 20 | $31 |
Sherborn Inn, 33 N. Main St. (Rtes. 16 & 27), Sherborn, 508-655-9521
M – All agree that the "refined setting" "takes you back 100 years" with its Colonial decor and "croquet matches on the lawn"; beyond that, fans applaud the inn's Sunday brunch and "carefully prepared food", while the minority says it's "run amateurishly" and "the food leaves a lot to be desired at the price."

Shilla/S | 16 | 11 | 15 | $19 |
95 Winthrop St. (bet. JFK & Brattle Sts.), Cambridge, 547-7971
U – Expect no more than "decent, standard" Korean and Japanese "food in the gloom", and this Harvard Square spot may work for you; prices are "reasonable" and the service, while "cool", is fairly efficient.

Shogun*/S | 18 | 14 | 14 | $18 |
1385 Washington St. (Elm St.), West Newton, 965-6699
U – "Nice, simple Japanese food" carries the day at this West Newton "neighborhood jewel"; it has the same "boring menu" you'll find at most Japanese spots but that doesn't make it any less "pleasant"; "slow service."

Siam Cuisine/SM | 21 | 17 | 19 | $17 |
961 Commonwealth Ave. (Gaffney St.), Allston, 254-4335
U – "One of the better Thais" has a reputation for its dependability and "great presentation"; despite qualms about the "too pink and green" interior, most surveyors like the feeling of being in an authentic Thai dining room.

Sibel | – | – | – | M |
100 Peterborough St. (Kilmarnock St.), 267-7346
Huge portions of Caribbean food from an unusually creative kitchen, a lovely staff and an immaculate if plain room would normally pack in the hordes, but being hidden behind Fenway Park means that not everyone knows this place; don't worry – they will soon enough, so better get there now.

Skewers, The/SMX | 14 | 7 | 11 | $12 |
92 Mt. Auburn St. (JFK St.), Cambridge, 491-3079
U – As long as you know what you're getting yourself into, this "excellent" Middle Eastern offers possibly the "best bargain in Cambridge"; you get "huge quantities" of food "very heavy on the garlic" at rock-bottom prices, served in a "hole-in-the-wall"; if this isn't your style, you'll find it "greasy and vulgar."

Boston | F | D | S | C |

SKIPJACK'S/SM | 21 | 18 | 19 | $24 |

199 Clarendon St. (Pearl St.), 536-3500
2 Brookline Place (off Boylston St., Rte. 9), Brookline, 232-8887

M – Everyone compares this pair of seafooderies, one way or another, to Legal – whether they're "right behind" Boston's most popular chain or they "blow Legal away" is a subjective call; virtues include a "good exotic fish selection" prepared creatively, "unusually helpful servers", cleanliness and "the best rolls ever"; demerits are for noise levels and prices.

Sol Azteca/SM | 21 | 18 | 18 | $21 |

914A Beacon St. (bet. Park Dr. & St. Mary's St.), Brookline, 262-0909
75 Union St. (bet. Beacon St. & Langley Rd.), Newton Centre, 964-0920

U – If it's not the "absolute best Mexican" in Boston, it's very close; "consistently excellent", the Brookline original has the "same old menu" and "cramped but comfortable atmosphere" it has had for years; the Newton Centre cafe is new.

Sorrento's | 20 | 13 | 17 | $15 |

86 Peterborough St. (bet. Kilmarnock & Jersey Sts.), 424-7070

M – The "exceptional rolls" are one of the few things surveyors agree on regarding this Fenway-area Italian "storefront"; fans point to "the best pizza in town" and "great pasta" and to the availability of takeout if you don't like the decor; foes say "three strikes, it's out."

Spaghetti Club, The | 15 | 13 | 13 | $19 |

93 Winthrop St. (bet. JFK & Dunlap Sts.), Cambridge, 576-1210

U – Although a smattering of surveyors have kind words for the pasta at this Harvard Square Northern Italian, to most it's an "expensive, pretentious pick-up joint" where the noise is unbearable for anyone over 25, the "chairs are uncomfortable" and the food is "nothing special."

SPINNAKER ITALIA | 16 | 24 | 18 | $25 |

Hyatt Regency Hotel, 575 Memorial Dr. (Amesberry St.), Cambridge, 492-1234

M – To "take a spin around Boston", head for this "tres romantique" revolving room that illustrates the maxim that "restaurants with a view always have mediocre food"; it's worth going for drinks or the "great brunch", and there's hope for the food – according to some, the recent switch to Northern Italian fare is a success.

Boston | F | D | S | C |

Sports Depot, The/SM | 14 | 16 | 14 | $15 |
(fka Allston Depot)
353 Cambridge St. (Harvard St.), Allston, 783-2300
M – Although "food remains a secondary feature" of this 30-TV suburban sports bar, its ratings – still admittedly unimpressive – have risen since our last Survey; "best for swilling beer and watching ball games", it has developed a line of "good bar appetizers."

Stage Deli/S | 16 | 12 | 13 | $16 |
725 Boylston St. (bet. Exeter & Fairfield Sts.), 859-9747
275 Tremont St. (near Stuart St.), 523-3354
M – The addition of a Boylston Street location results from the success of the original Tremont Street branch of the famous New York deli, but success is a relative thing – Bostonians who haven't had better sing its praises, but the rest consider it proof that "NY delis don't travel well."

Star of Siam/SM | 20 | 11 | 16 | $15 |
93 Church St. (Stuart St.), 451-5236
U – This Back Bay Thai with "excellent pad thai" and "tacky Oriental decor" doesn't quite make it into the first rank, but its excellent value assures it of a loyal clientele; our raters ask only that the good-natured staff would learn a bit more English and "clean up, please."

Stars Ocean* | 23 | 10 | 17 | $15 |
70-72 Kilmarnock St. (bet. Peterborough & Queensberry Sts.), 236-0161
U – Though not widely known to our surveyors, this Fenway-area Chinese wins high praise for its "fresh cheap eats"; "friendly and never crowded", it would be "wonderful" even if it cost a little more; either turn a blind eye to the surroundings or use their very quick delivery service.

St. Botolph/SM | 19 | 19 | 19 | $30 |
99 St. Botolph St. (W. Newton St.), 266-3030
M – A "South End stalwart", this Contemporary American is "not as dependable as it once was", but is "still quite good"; service remains "discreet and well-paced", though waiters may "push items that aren't moving"; P.S. many surveyors prefer the cafe downstairs.

St. Cloud/LSM | 22 | 21 | 20 | $31 |
557 Tremont St. (Clarendon St.), 353-0202
U – This American Nouvelle restaurant still "does most things right", holding on to its "glittery crowd" with "interesting food", a stylish "high-tech" setting and "terrific Sunday a la carte brunch", and "cool service"; the main drawback is that "the suburbs have discovered it."

Boston | F | D | S | C |

Steak in the Neighborhood, A | 14 | 14 | 15 | $18 |
Sheraton Boston Hotel and Towers, 39 Dalton St. (bet. Boylston St. & Huntington Ave.), 262-1822
M – "Neighborhood playground" near the Prudential Building with "huge portions of greasy bar food", a "rowdy" "college atmosphere", waiters who've never heard of bearnaise sauce, and "reasonable prices"; some find this "festive", others "forgettable."

Stellina's/S | 22 | 13 | 19 | $24 |
52 Galen St. (Water St.), Watertown, 924-9475
U – With a recent move to larger quarters, this Watertown Italian has consolidated its popularity; now there's room to enjoy the "honest Italian food" without the decibel level of the original; service remains "attentive" and most people still find it "quite reasonable."

Stockyard, The | 15 | 13 | 15 | $19 |
135 Market St. (bet. N. Beacon St. & Birmingham Pkwy.), Brighton, 782-4700
M – A steak house that's known for "sensational prime rib" but little else; "quantity, but not so much quality" is the name of the game, with the "wait staff only fair" and cleanliness a problem; the dearth of competition in the area makes it more viable.

Streets Cafe* | 14 | 9 | 15 | $9 |
226 Newbury St. (bet. Exeter & Fairfield Sts.), 267-5567
U – This Back Bay Vegetarian-Italian's "good, hearty soups" and "ordinary sandwiches", as well as its "great location", make it a useful lunch stop, but not much more.

Sultan's Kitchen | 22 | 9 | 14 | $11 |
72 Broad St. (bet. Milk & Franklin Sts.), 338-7819
U – An asset to any neighborhood, this "excellent" Turkish lunch spot is a revelation in its Downtown location; despite the "sparse self-service atmosphere", the "wonderful", "quick", "good value" cuisine causes a lot of people to "adore this place", e.g. "I was raised on Middle Eastern food and this rivals my childhood memories."

Sunset Cafe/S | 18 | 14 | 18 | $17 |
851 Cambridge St. (Inman Sq.), Cambridge, 547-2938
U – Inman Square's "local Portuguese community diner" specializes in "very tasty", homey fare served in "outlandish portions"; add "terrific people-watching" and "great weekend singalongs in Portuguese", and you've got "excellent value for money"; P.S. the bar will "make you feel old if you're over 25."

Boston | F | D | S | C |

Sunset Grill & Tap | 16 | 13 | 15 | $14 |
130 Brighton Ave. (Harvard St.), Allston, 254-1331
U – A "beer lover's heaven" with an "unbelievable selection", this Allston tap room also features "surprisingly good specials" along with its "smoky, noisy" "college ambiance"; service is too laid-back for its own good and funkiness is elevated to an art form, but habitues couldn't care less.

Sushi-Nagoya* | 15 | 12 | 18 | $16 |
426 Harvard St. (bet. Thorndike & Coolidge Sts.), Brookline, 731-5500
U – The sushi is "good" (though some argue it "could be fresher") and the bargain prices at this Brookline hole-in-the-wall make it even more worth knowing; "communicating is sometimes a problem."

Ta Chien/LSM | 17 | 12 | 16 | $15 |
900 Beacon St. (bet. Park Dr. & St. Mary's St.), 247-3666
U – "Uninspired but reliable", this dowdy Kenmore Square Chinese may be "inexpensive" – which probably accounts for all the students – but to our critics it's only "slightly above average"; if you must go, do it at lunchtime and ignore the service.

Taiwan Taste* | 17 | 13 | 21 | $15 |
10 Tyler St. (bet. Kneeland & Beach Sts.), 542-5857
U – This Chinatown spot for regional Taiwanese and other Chinese cuisines isn't well known, but those who have stopped by have nothing but praise for the "very nice people" and what a few are already calling "the best Chinese around"; worth keeping tabs on.

TAKESHIMA | 24 | 17 | 22 | $20 |
308 Harvard St. (Babcock St.), Brookline, 566-0200
U – Most everyone goes for the "consistently wonderful and fresh" sushi at this "clean, attractive" Brookline Japanese; despite a few qualms about the service, a great majority of respondents praise the variety of the menu and "would hate to have all of Boston know about it – it's already tough enough to get in."

Tam O'Shanter/SMX | 19 | 10 | 16 | $18 |
1648 Beacon St. (near Washington St., Washington Sq.), Brookline, 277-0982
U – For "yummy food in a yukky atmosphere", this Brookline down-home American fills the bill; "terrific breads" and "great stews" offset the "dark, noisy", "kind of greasy" setting; if you prefer to "enjoy your food without smoke and dancers in your face", go early, before the fine rock and blues bands begin.

Boston | **F** | **D** | **S** | **C** |

Tandoor House/SM | 17 | 13 | 17 | $17 |
(fka Ashoka)
991 Massachusetts Ave. (bet. Dana & Elery Sts.),
Cambridge, 661-9001
M – "Not the best" on the Mass Avenue Indian strip, this Central Square spot's "inconsistent" food in a "plain setting" too often "misses", but it's cheap and friendly enough to win its share of regard.

Tapas/SM | 16 | 15 | 16 | $21 |
2067 Massachusetts Ave. (Walden St.), Cambridge, 576-2240
M – The consensus is that "something's missing" at this Cambridge Spaniard known for its eponymous plates of appetizers; though it offers "welcome variety" and can be "a good change of pace", many find the fare "mediocre" and the room "run-down"; plus, "those tiny plates get expensive."

Taste of India/SM | 19 | 11 | 18 | $18 |
91 Bigelow Ave. (near Mt. Auburn St.), Watertown, 926-1606
U – This "great neighborhood find" with "decent" Indian food and "caring and fast" service makes for a "comfortable place to linger"; you may find better in Cambridge, but you might not consider the trip worth it.

Tatsukichi/SM | 22 | 19 | 19 | $24 |
189 State St. (near Atlantic Ave.), 720-2468
U – "Japanese food so good even the Japanese eat here" sums up the enthusiasm about this "consistently good" Faneuil Hall-area restaurant; the atmosphere is "quiet and calming" and the service, although "a bit slow", is very friendly; fans rave about the "very fresh" and "creative" sushi, and the karaoke singalongs are "fun!!"

Ten Huntington | 20 | 20 | 20 | $33 |
Westin Hotel, 10 Huntington St. (Dartmouth St., Copley Pl.), 424-7429
M – "A little too pretentious" but "good for a hotel", this Westin dining room doesn't seem to hit a consistent groove; sometimes the service is "impeccable", at other times "take-it-or-leave-it"; the traditional American food, likewise, ranges from "excellent" to "passable"; kids go for the grill-it-yourself hot rocks.

Boston

| | F | D | S | C |

TGI Friday's/LSM | 15 | 16 | 16 | $16 |
26 Exeter St. (Newbury St.), 266-9040
M – Nobody expects much from this joint with old-timey decor, but it's "very popular", forever filled with college students and kids celebrating birthdays; the burgers and onion rings can be good, ditto with salads, but it's the "upbeat" crowd and "fun" atmosphere, not the food, that keep it full.

Thai Cuisine/SM | 21 | 15 | 18 | $16 |
14A Westland Ave. (near Mass. Ave.), 262-1485
U – To lovers of Thai-style curries, this standby is "the only good place pre-Symphony"; at those times, it's "small, crowded and can be a bit rushed", but usually maintains its "serene setting" and "reliable, solid" fare.

Thai House/SM | 21 | 16 | 19 | $17 |
1033 Commonwealth Ave. (across from Babcock St.), Brighton, 787-4242
U – "Unimposing but well-done", this underdecorated Brighton Thai is bound to be a favorite, especially "if you like garlic"; our surveyors praise the cleanliness, the prices, the "good, good service" and the efficient takeout; overall, "one of the best" of its kind.

Thornton's* | 13 | 5 | 12 | $11 |
150 Huntington Ave. (W. Newton Ave.), 267-6336
U – Strictly a neighborhood place known for its sidewalk cafe, this South End's American fare makes it "great for a local brunch, but don't go out of your way"; the food's nothing special, but the price is right.

Tien's Thai | 23 | 17 | 20 | $19 |
12 School St. (Mt. Pleasant St.), Marblehead, 639-1334
U – Who cares if "the best Thai around" is "in an unlikely town"? – its "excellent, fresh, light and delicious" flavors would be welcome anywhere; although the staff's English is rudimentary, they're genuinely lovely people, and if there's "no decor, at least it's not tacky."

Tim's Tavern | 18 | 9 | 12 | $14 |
329 Columbus Ave. (near Dartmouth St.), 247-7894
U – To fans of this "back-home bar and grill", "every neighborhood deserves a dive this good", with its "huge hamburgers", "good, cheap food" and "Southern hospitality"; not everyone gets a charge out of the surroundings, but overall, it's a stellar example of its genre.

Boston | F | D | S | C |

Top of the Hub/SM | 13 | 22 | 15 | $28 |
Prudential Center (bet. Boylston St. & Huntington Ave.),
536-1775
*U – For most, dining here is "just like being on an
airplane – nice view, rotten food"; though the "staff is
very friendly", the room "needs a face-lift" and the tab
is high for what you get; our critics advise going for the
"adequate" brunch to get your scenery fix.*

Troyka* | 16 | 12 | 13 | $13 |
1154 Massachusetts Ave. (Arrow St.), 864-7476
*M – This tiny, "depressing" Harvard Square spot
features respectable "Russian food with Soviet service",
as well as "small portions" and a "claustrophobic
atmosphere"; though some find the "earth mother
food" somewhat "interesting", most say "nyet."*

Turner Fisheries/LSM | 20 | 18 | 18 | $27 |
Westin Hotel, 10 Huntington Ave., (Dartmouth St.,
Copley Pl.), 424-7425, 262-9600
*M – Despite arguably "the best clam chowder in
Boston", this hotel seafoodery "seems to be losing its
edge"; a "lively bar" and "above average" fare don't
quite compensate for the "indifferent service", "dull
setting" and high-ish prices; it's still "dependable", but
there's "no heart."*

29 Newbury/SM | 17 | 17 | 14 | $25 |
29 Newbury St. (bet. Arlington & Berkeley Sts.), 536-0290
*M – This fashionable Back Bay Contemporary
American can still claim "awesome people-watching",
but the "snooty food and service" have become old
hat; "erratic but occasionally brilliant", even "their
downscaling didn't help."*

224 Boston St. | – | – | – | M |
224 Boston St. (bet. Andrew Sq. & Edward Everett Sq.),
Dorchester, 265-1217
*Recently discovered by people outside its Dorchester
neighborhood, this highly Eclectic casual cafe – which
serves everything from excellent burgers to Caribbean-
style stewed goat – is a lot of fun; it offers a little bit of
everything, including changing art displays and a
sprightly mix of live music.*

Boston | **F** | **D** | **S** | **C** |

Union Grille | 23 | 15 | 22 | $19 |
208 Rantoul St. (parallel to Cabot St.), Beverly, 508-927-2028
U – Forget the "blah atmosphere" and turn your attention to the "consistently wonderful" kitchen at this first-rate New American grill that's great before the North Shore Music Theater; to avoid the "long lines" caused by the no-reservations policy, arrive early.

Union Oyster House/SM | 16 | 17 | 15 | $22 |
41 Union St. (bet. Hanover & North Sts.), 227-2750
M – Local advice regarding this venerable "tourist trap" is to head straight for the "superb raw bar" and "avoid the rest"; "way past its prime", the kitchen takes "too many shortcuts" while the waiters seem to do the opposite; "go at an off-time", however, and you'll be in a position to enjoy the "olde Boston" atmosphere.

Union Street Cafe | 16 | 14 | 15 | $19 |
1017-R Union St. (bet. Langley Rd. & Centre St.), Newton Centre, 964-6684
M – "Go for the outdoor cafe" and the "artistic decor" of this suburban Internationalist, say surveyors, who agree on little else; while some have kind words for the brunch, others find dining here "not memorable" and suspect "it gets by on reputation and location."

UPSTAIRS AT THE PUDDING | 24 | 19 | 21 | $42 |
10 Holyoke St. (bet. Mass. Ave. & Holyoke Ctr., Harvard Sq.), Cambridge, 864-1933
U – Improving food ratings mean "you can tell when a chef loves to cook" at this "slightly too Harvardy" "special occasion place"; the "excellent" and "very innovative" Continental-Northern Italian fare, though "overpriced", helps make it "a great spot to entertain people"; your appreciation of things Ivy will determine whether you find the atmosphere "lovely" or "shabby", the service "terrific" or "atrocious."

Venetian Gardens | 17 | 13 | 18 | $18 |
1269 Massachusetts Ave. (Columbia Rd.), 436-9327
U – This landmark red-sauce Italian "has gone upscale" and Northernized somewhat of late, and for some old fans it "has been ruined"; still, the new owner's "trying hard" and most customers continue to appreciate the "cheap eats."

Boston | F | D | S | C |

Venus Seafood in the Rough | 17 | 13 | 10 | $14 |
88 Sleeper St. (Northern Ave., over Northern Ave. Bridge), 426-3388
U – Almost everyone considers this new waterfront fish shack a "great idea" that "Boston needed"; though it may be "a little too close to the harbor smell", kids love the "fun, salt and sea" and no one seems to mind that the self-service on paper plates lacks elegance and the food is simplicity itself.

Verona* | 20 | 11 | 17 | $16 |
18 Mt. Auburn St. (Watertown Sq.), Watertown, 926-0010
M – Few have ventured into this sensibly priced Watertown Italian, but from those who have we get reports of a "wonderful neighborhood restaurant" that's short on atmosphere but great for families.

Veronique | 20 | 22 | 21 | $30 |
20 Chapel St. (Longwood Ave.), Brookline, 731-4800
M – This newly reopened Brookline Classic French charmer "looks better than it tastes" to our surveyors, who preferred the old (more convenient, but less lovely) Coolidge Corner location; whether the "mellow", "romantic setting" wows you or not, the standard, smoothly executed French cuisine isn't likely to improve your opinion, though the "sophisticated wine list" may.

Via Veneto/LS | 19 | 17 | 19 | $26 |
283 Causeway St. (N. Washington St.), 742-4142
M – Convenient to Boston Garden, this Italian yearling has had a burst of energy in the kitchen of late that will certainly improve its food ratings; while often "spotty" and "oversauced" in the past, in the last year our critics say it has become "surprisingly good"; once "perfect for a pie" before a game, now the entire menu's worth exploring.

Victoria Diner | 17 | 11 | 18 | $14 |
1024 Massachusetts Ave. (Shirley St., Newmarket Sq.), 442-5965
U – Not exactly a culinary star, this standard-issue American diner remains the place for "good, consistent food" that's not great, but plentiful; it's good for "breakfast at 3 AM", when you're less likely to notice the humdrum surroundings.

Boston

| | F | D | S | C |

Victoria Station/SM | 13 | 14 | 14 | $19 |
64 Sleeper St. (off Congress St.), 542-7771
U – Perhaps the kindest comment our critics can muster for this Waterfront branch of the national chain, with its "Pepsi Generation" menu, is that it's "almost ok"; otherwise, we hear about "blah food", a "tiresome atmosphere", "inept service" and "mass-produced" decor; still, in its way it's reliable, the salad bar has fans and kids love the place.

Viet Restaurant*/SM | 21 | 11 | 17 | $15 |
25 Tyler St. (near Kneeland St.), 350-6615
U – This "delicious, fresh and peaceful place" would be Boston's top Vietnamese if more people had voted on it; nonetheless, those who know it give it high marks for reasonable prices and "trying very hard."

Villa Francesca | 19 | 16 | 16 | $25 |
150 Richmond St. (bet. Hanover & North Sts.), 367-2948
M – "Ample portions" of "standard North End Italian fare" served by a singing staff explains the prevailing view that "popularity exceeds quality" at this old standby; still, it's "upbeat and friendly" food is "good enough" to keep 'em coming.

Village Fish, The/SMX | 22 | 12 | 16 | $20 |
22 Harvard St. (near Washington St.), Brookline Village, 566-3474 (FISH)
U – Another "noisy, loud, crowded" seafoodery specializing in "excellent fish, simply prepared" and realistically priced, this local favorite does what it does quite well; expect lines at peak times, off-and-on service, and "impersonal atmosphere", but "great calamari."

Village Smokehouse, The | 16 | 12 | 14 | $17 |
1 Harvard St. (Washington St.), Brookline Village, 566-3782
M – Rib-lovers find this "down-and-dirty" BBQ joint "good, messy and convivial", not to mention cheap, while those opposed to "large portions of protein and fat" consider it "poisonous"; maybe it's not the best BBQ in town, but with so few options it'll do nicely, especially if you've got kids.

Boston | F | D | S | C |

Vin & Eddie's | 23 | 17 | 20 | $30 |
1400 Bedford St. (Rte. 18 bet. Rtes. 58 & 139), Abington, 871-1469
U – "A real sleeper" on the South Shore is this "top-shelf" Italian roadhouse with "no atmosphere", but "pleasant" people in charge; our participants like not only the "wonderfully prepared" food, but also that "they change the menu frequently"; add a "good wine list" and it's small wonder that the most common complaint is that you've got "too long to wait."

Vinny Marino's* | 16 | 13 | 19 | $18 |
4161 Washington St. (near Roslindale Sq.), Roslindale, 325-6960
U – This "very friendly" combination Italian-BBQ-Middle Eastern spot has a following in its area; though its "revolving chefs" assure inconsistency and the "dark atmosphere" can be forbidding, they try hard to please and are especially nice to families.

Warren Tavern | 13 | 22 | 16 | $22 |
2 Pleasant St. (Main St.), Charlestown, 241-8142
M – An "old Boston feeling" permeates this Colonial-era standby, but the food has deserted it; the sandwiches and homemade chips have their champions, but for most the "quaint New England surroundings" are best enjoyed for "drinks only."

Washington Street Bar & Grill | 20 | 20 | 18 | $20 |
259 Washington St. (bet. Atlantic & Pleasant Sts.), Marblehead, 639-4141
U – A "fun spot" for "original" Southwest-style food, this "casual" place mixes "good value" and a "pleasant atmosphere" to create the sort of place that's a real asset in Marblehead, or anywhere.

Weylu's/LSM | 18 | 20 | 17 | $19 |
254 Summer St. (2 blocks from South Station), 423-0243
334 N. Pearl St. (Oak St.), Brockton, 587-8100
Rte. 1 (near Rte. 93), Saugus, 233-1632
East India Mall, Church St. (near Essex St.), Salem, 745-4200
M – These Chinese with "elaborate decor" and "better than average" food are "overly ambitious"; in trying to do too much, they produce kitsch and crowds, but little consistency, and service has noticeably suffered.

Boston

| | F | D | S | C |

White Rainbow | 23 | 21 | 21 | $33 |
65 Main St. (Rogers St.), Gloucester, 508-281-0017
U – A "rare find", this "very good" Nouvelle American cafe is a much-appreciated "romantic rendezvous" for Cape Ann, even if "the staff is snobby" and the menu a trifle "boring"; let's face it, it's "superior" in every way to the area competition.

Willow Pond Kitchen | 13 | 11 | 14 | $14 |
745 Lexington Rd. (Rte. 9A, near Hanscom Field), Concord, 508-369-6529
M – This old-time dive looks like a taxidermist's waiting room and serves up ultra-cheap lobsters and seafood that drive people to extreme reactions; to those who love it, it's "the last taste of old New England", with "waitresses who yell at you" and "fried everything"; to others, the majority, it's "below any standard"; both camps have a point – "it's authentic, but so is heartburn."

Winery Restaurant, The/SM | 13 | 16 | 14 | $23 |
Lewis Wharf (Atlantic & Commercial Sts), 423-3994
M – "Another great location wasted", this "impersonal" American "for thirtysomething types" mixes "spectacular views" and a "nice summer patio" with food most find "a cliche"; ok as an after-work spot.

Wursthaus, The | 13 | 12 | 13 | $16 |
4 JFK St. (Brattle St.), Cambridge, 491-7110
U – Ok, so this Harvard Square "institution" isn't "the worst restaurant in the world", even if its "heavy, salty" German fare lays in the stomach like buckshot and the "inelegant, common" room is so dark you can barely see your hand in front of your face; just "drink lotsa beer, forget the food" and the spiteful service, and soak up the collegiate atmosphere.

Yangtze River/SM | 17 | 13 | 16 | $17 |
25 Depot Square (Mass. Ave. at Lexington Ctr.), Lexington, 861-6030
M – The kitchen usually satisfies at this Lexington Chinese that "used to be better"; it gets by on swift though not-so-cheerful service and a popular dinner buffet that's "pretty edible, considering"; the place is popular enough to attract crowds.

Yelena | – | – | – | M |
298 Washington St. (Brighton Center), Brighton, 787-0037
In a Brighton neighborhood whose Russian population is growing rapidly, this is felt to be slightly peculiar, but one of the most authentic new spots around; very popular with locals, it offers a fun atmosphere that, late in the evening, can very easily burst into song.

Boston | F | D | S | C |

Yenching Palace | 14 | 9 | 15 | $14 |
671 Boylston St. (bet. Exeter & Dartmouth Sts., Copley Sq.), 266-9367
U – "Chinese food for white folks" means "too much MSG", fast service and a very predictable menu, but not – surprisingly – a lot of attention to cleanliness; it's reliable and cheap, but don't expect much.

Zuma Tex-Mex Cafe | 17 | 18 | 17 | $19 |
Faneuil Hall Marketplace (North Market Bldg.), 367-9114
M – Young, eclectic and somewhat disorganized, this Southwestern grill is "surprisingly good for the Faneuil Hall area", where the competition is feeble; nevertheless, the funky buzz and the novelty of the cuisine – not to mention the sane prices, which have just plunged – compensate for not-quite-greatness.

TOP RESTAURANTS IN CAPE COD, MARTHA'S VINEYARD, NANTUCKET, RHODE ISLAND, NEW HAMPSHIRE AND MAINE

Cape Cod, Martha's Vineyard and Nantucket

| F | D | S | C |

Black Dog Tavern | 21 | 18 | 19 | $21 |
Beach St. Extension (Vineyard Haven Harbor),
Martha's Vineyard, 508-693-9223
U – This "fun, earthy" place is responsible for the "greatest breakfast anywhere" – or, at least, on the Vineyard – "if you can stand the wait"; at dinnertime it's just as "relaxed and convivial" (and just as genially "grungy"), but prices seem less reasonable somehow, even with the BYO policy; still, many feel it "completes a trip to the Vineyard", and the T-shirts it sells are a part of yuppie uniforms all over the country.

CHANTICLEER | 27 | 26 | 24 | $50 |
9 New St. (Siasconset Center), Nantucket, 508-257-6231
U – "Absolutely lovely" in every way is this Nantucket Classic French with its "extremely romantic and secluded" setting, "clubby atmosphere", "fabulous wine list", "purposefully snobbish" service and "super food"; though a few find it "pompous" and feel it has "dropped a notch", the vast majority think it "really special", "almost worth robbing a bank" to meet the stiff tab.

CHILLINGSWORTH | 27 | 27 | 26 | $50 |
2449 Main St. (Rte. 6A), Brewster, 508-896-3640
U – Its food ratings confirm that it's "as close to perfect" as the Cape – and maybe even Boston – can be; "superb", "creative", "top-notch" Nouvelle French cooking, "fastidious" and "very formal service" and an atmosphere of "casual elegance" point to "very high standards" overall; granted, it's "as expensive as it gets", but "you get what you pay for."

Ciro & Sal's | 21 | 18 | 18 | $27 |
4 Kiley Court (Commercial St.), Provincetown, 508-487-0049
M – While it's unquestionably "a step above a red-sauce joint", this "solid" P-town Italian is probably a little "too touristy" to merit an unqualified recommendation; "funky and crowded", its kitchen can deliver, but doesn't do it consistently, and service is likewise variable; there's often a "long wait even with reservations" at peak times.

Cape Cod, Martha's Vineyard and Nantucket

	F	D	S	C

CRANBERRY MOOSE, THE | 24 | 21 | 22 | $41 |

43 Main St. (Rte. 6A, exit 7, near Willow St.),
Yarmouthport, 508-362-3501
U – While ratings have slipped a bit from the last Survey, the great majority of respondents still feel this Contemporary American is "a winner" by virtue of its "adventurous entrees", "smartly paced" service and "very pleasant atmosphere"; a few, though, find the place too "cute, cute, cute", the wait staff "sloppy" (especially on Saturday nights in season) and the menu overambitious.

Galley* | 23 | 26 | 19 | $46 |

Cliffside Beach, Nantucket, 508-228-9641
U – If "very romantic" beachside dining is your thing, this Nantucket Eclectic may well delight you; the food, while very good, isn't quite up to the "wonderful location", but "if you're in the mood" you'll make small allowances.

High Brewster* | 24 | 25 | 24 | $42 |

Satucket Rd. (bet. Airline & Stonybrook Rds.), Brewster, 508-896-3636
U – More people ought to patronize this "truly spectacular" outpost of "American cuisine at its best", say the select group who know it; with its "superb setting" and "homey New England food", it's surprising it's not more widely known.

Le Grenier* | 22 | 20 | 22 | $34 |

Upper Main St. (1½ blocks from the ferry), Vineyard Haven, Martha's Vineyard, 508-693-4906
U – Notwithstanding its ongoing popularity, there are indications that this Vineyard French may be slipping a bit; the "food can be inconsistent", the sauces "a little too heavy", the "service careless at lunch" – however, solid ratings and good values suggest these flaws are far from fatal.

L'Etoile at the Charlotte Inn* | 25 | 28 | 23 | $45 |

Charlotte Inn, 27 S. Summer St. (1 block from Main St.), Edgartown, Martha's Vineyard, 508-627-5187
U – The early returns on this Vineyard newcomer are overwhelmingly favorable; respondents find the "atmosphere wonderful", the offerings on the "unusual" Contemporary French menu "superbly done"; the staff can on occasion come across as "haughty", but that's the only thing approaching a complaint.

| Cape Cod, Martha's Vineyard and Nantucket | F | D | S | C |

Marshside* | 20 | 14 | 19 | $18 |
28 Bridge St. (off Rte. 6A), E. Dennis, 508-385-4010
U – Not much more than a "glorified coffee shop", this "real family restaurant" does a booming breakfast business because "they try hard" and they get it right; lunch and dinner aren't quite as successful, though the chicken puff pie and seafood stew are both justly famous.

REGATTA OF COTUIT AT THE CROCKER HOUSE | 25 | 25 | 23 | $42 |
4631 Falmouth Rd. (near Rte. 130), Cotuit, 508-428-5715
U – There's little but praise for the "friendly welcome", the "romantic, Colonial atmosphere" and the "ever-changing, interesting menu" at this "great meeting place" on the Cape – and, what's more, "the owners know their wine"; though occasionally the wait staff can seem haughty, it's almost always "a delightful dining experience."

REGATTA OF FALMOUTH BY THE SEA | 24 | 23 | 23 | $41 |
217 Clinton Ave. (near Scranton Ave.), Falmouth, 508-548-5400
U – Although its overall ratings are slightly lower, this sibling of the Regatta of Cotuit gets high marks for a setting with "a great view of all the boats and activity" as much for its "usually delicious" food; slightly more casual and less costly than Cotuit, it's a worthy companion.

Second Story* | 22 | 20 | 21 | $38 |
1 S. Beach St. (bet. Steamboat Wharf & South Beach), Nantucket, 508-228-3471
M – Whether you find its "recent trend toward more exotic", Asian flavorings an inspiration or a "disappointment", you'll certainly agree it's one of the most adventurous spots on Nantucket; it'll be either "fabulous" or "not worth it", depending on your taste for such adventures.

Straight Wharf* | 25 | 23 | 25 | $35 |
Straight Wharf, Nantucket, 508-228-1095
U – "Superb, dignified and lovely", this is "the Nantucket favorite" for some surveyors; they love the "excellent location", the service and "the best food on the island", and wish only that the place did a better job of dealing with crowds; "the bar's a good choice for lunch, too."

Cape Cod, Martha's Vineyard and Nantucket | F | D | S | C |

Summerhouse, The | - | - | - | E |

Ocean Ave., Siasconset, Nantucket, 508-257-9976
On a summer night, this lively Contemporary American located in a picturebook villlage can be "magical", with its bustling bar scene and "romantic" setting filled with flowers; there's more than atmosphere, though – the cooking, centered around first-rate seafood, is tasty and imaginative without being precious.

TOPPERS | 23 | 25 | 22 | $46 |

Wauwinet Inn, end of Wauwinet Rd., Nantucket, 508-228-0145
M – "The island's new star" throws a "Brahmin garden party" at dinner time that fans find "transcendent"; despite the "great ambiance", some report that the New American "food is not always fab", but more say it's "just about the best on Nantucket", and well worth the tariff.

21 FEDERAL | 25 | 23 | 22 | $42 |

21 Federal St. (Oak St.), Nantucket, 508-228-2121
U – A significant rise in food ratings indicates that this "stylish" New American has reached its potential; surveyors praise the "excellent", "innovative" kitchen, the "handsome" Colonial setting and the "professional service", and suggest "reserving well in advance – it's worth it"; the famous Washington, D.C. restaurant is an offshoot.

Rhode Island

AL FORNO | 27 | 21 | 23 | $34 |

577 S. Main St. (behind Corliss Landing), Providence, 401-272-7980
U – "They practice alchemy, not cooking", say the many adoring fans of this Northern Italian that, somewhat perversely, refuses to take reservations; but as long as the "heaping portions" ("it's cheap if you share") of "delectable" fare arrive at the table and the service remains "very knowledgeable and warm", no one cares much about the waits; chef-owners Johanne Kileen and George Germon have won nationwide reputations for their food that's well worth a trip, even a long one.

ANGEL'S | 25 | 21 | 22 | $37 |

125 N. Main St. (Meeting St.), Providence, 401-273-0310
M – The essence of Providence Cool, this Internationalist offers up "trendy food at killer prices" to a "hip Rhode Island School of Design crowd"; however, while most respondents proclaim the kitchen "superb", with "the best steak in Providence", a few deem it "a poor copy of better restaurants."

| **Rhode Island** | F | D | S | C |

Black Pearl | 21 | 19 | 20 | $29 |
Bannister's Wharf, Newport, 401-846-5264
M – There's a great deal of enthusiasm for the "super chowder" at this wharfside Newporter, but the rest of the Continental menu, while "above average", never gets much better than "amazingly adequate"; though perhaps it's "not as good as its reputation", the combination of "good, solid, dependable fare", "people-watching" and "great view of the harbor" make it "worth a visit."

Blue Point Oyster Bar | 22 | 15 | 18 | $32 |
99 N. Main St. (top of Elizabeth St.), Providence, 401-272-6145
U – You'll get "sore fins" from the "rather uncomfortable" seating at this "outstanding, creative" seafoodery, but most feel the "great seafood" and "excellent wine list" (including "a fine selection of chardonnays") compensate nicely; still, it does seem "awfully pricey" for the setting.

Caserta's Pizza | 22 | 9 | 12 | $11 |
121 Spruce St. (bet. Acorn & Dean Sts.), Providence, 401-272-3618
U – This admitted "dump" has some of the "best pizza north of New Haven", with "fresh tomatoes and cheese"; the rest of the menu is perhaps best described as "bastardized Italian food."

Clarke Cooke House | 19 | 20 | 18 | $31 |
Bannisters Wharf, Newport, 401-849-2900
M – "Filled with yuppies and upscale sailors", this spot "right on Newport Harbor" may be "good for traditional" regional fare, but the kitchen ultimately has "nothing interesting" up its sleeve; the "awfully slow service" is only fitting at a place so "full of itself", but the burgers, chowder and stuffed clams keep many satisfied.

Great House, The | – | – | – | M |
2245 Post Rd. (¼ mile south of T.F. Green Airport), Warwick, 401-739-8600
Given its location in a turn-of-the-century mansion, the solid New England fare here is to be expected – the wild card is that there is also a well-executed Chinese menu (the owners are Chinese); the comfortable, antique-filled rooms and the generous portions make this a local favorite.

Rhode Island | F | D | S | C |

Hemenway's | 18 | 19 | 16 | $26 |
1 Old Stone Square (bet. S. Water & S. Main Sts.),
Providence, 401-351-8570
U – Providence's answer to Legal Sea Foods can be "heavenly" or "pedestrian", but one thing it certainly isn't is consistent; surveyors like the waterfront view better than the "slooow service."

Le Petite Auberge* | 23 | 20 | 21 | $40 |
19 Charles St. (bet. Washington Sq. & Marlboro St.),
Newport, 401-849-6669
U – The scattered returns on this Newport Country French are inconclusive, but we hear the cooking's "excellent."

LUCKY'S | 26 | 22 | 23 | $35 |
577 S. Main St. (behind Corliss Landing), Providence,
401-272-7980
U – This Provence-inspired bistro runs a close second to its sibling, Al Forno, for Providence's hearts and stomachs; although almost everything on the menu is "fabulous", the grilled pizzas in particular are "to swoon over"; choosing between this place and its older relation upstairs defines the term "golden problem."

Modern Diner* | 18 | 14 | 16 | $14 |
364 East Ave. (bet. Pleasant & Pawtucket Sts.),
Pawtucket, 401-726-8390
U – This "funky, trendy, down-at-the-mouth" art deco diner "could have been great", and its food sometimes is, but respondents feel it doesn't quite click.

Newport Grill | 21 | 18 | 20 | $28 |
1 Broadway (Washington Sq.), Newport, 401-847-8353
M – Most people are well pleased by this outstanding new grill that's "the least pretentious restaurant" in the vicinity; still, the "fresh, well-prepared" Mediterranean-Italian fare has occasional misses, and "very tight seating" and a no-reservations policy simply do not appeal to some Newporters.

Pot Au Feu | 23 | 21 | 22 | $31 |
44 Custom House St. (Weybosset St.), Providence,
401-273-8953
U – With a bistro downstairs and a more formal salon upstairs, this French spot has partisans for both; some prefer the "romantic, intimate" flavor of the salon, others the "casual atmosphere" downstairs; either way, it's a "consistent high-quality performer" without many soaring peaks, but few valleys either.

Rhode Island

| F | D | S | C |

Toscano's | 23 | 20 | 20 | $33 |
265 Atwells Ave. (DePasquale Plaza), Providence, 401-274-8820
M – An outpost of Boston's Ristorante Toscano, this Northern Italian suffers slightly from the comparison, though locals like the fact that it's "less pretentious than the Beantown version"; still, the fine, unusually authentic fare doesn't lose much in the transfer.

WHITE HORSE TAVERN | 23 | 25 | 24 | $39 |
Marlborough St. (Farewell St.), Newport, 401-849-3600
U – A "very well-kept" old tavern with an especially desirable fireplace for winter evenings, this Eclectic Newporter is "good, solid and dependable" in every way – in other words, perfectly New England; the food, short of being great, is far better than that of the local competition; the service is "impressive yet snobbish."

New Hampshire and Maine

Alberta's Cafe* | 23 | 19 | 20 | $19 |
21 Pleasant St. (bet. Danforth & Foke Sts.), Portland ME, 207-774-0016
U – It's "a great surprise" to find this "simply outstanding" Eclectic in Portland; the price you pay for the food isn't so much monetary, but in "crowds and slow service at the height of summer."

ARROWS | 26 | 25 | 24 | $39 |
Berwick St., Ogunquit ME, 207-361-1100
U – The "superb food" is on par with the "fantastic farmhouse setting" of this "very special" New American; it's worth the considerable (for Ogunquit) expense to choose from the "innovative menu" with Californian overtones; service is attentive almost to a fault; non-Bostonians recommend going "after Labor Day, when the tourists are gone."

BLUE STRAWBERY | 25 | 22 | 23 | $39 |
39 Ceres St. (off Bow St.), Portsmouth NH, 603-431-6420
M – The "well-prepared feasts" served family-style at mixed sittings at this Nouvelle American have gotten a bit less "gimmicky" and "ridiculous", letting the "excellent, inventive" cooking shine through; although it remains "too bizarre" or simply "too too" for some palates, it seems to have struck a good balance between innovation and recognizability.

New Hampshire and Maine | F | D | S | C |

Cape Neddick Inn | 23 | 23 | 21 | $31 |
Intersection of Rtes. 1 & 1A, Cape Neddick ME, 207-363-2899
U – Pricey for the area but "worth it", this "unusual", "charming", romantic Nouvelle American with a French flair is finding a loyal audience; although a few pronounce the sauces "fussy", the majority view is that the "innovative menu" works perfectly.

D'Artagnan* | 25 | 21 | 24 | $39 |
13 Dartmouth College Hwy. (Rte. 10), Lyme NH, 603-795-2137
U – Most think "there's no better restaurant in New Hampshire" than this Nouvelle French; with a "friendly and delightful" chef (who also does a "superb" job in the kitchen), you might not even notice that the surroundings aren't quite up to the food; a minority considers it "overrated."

Promises To Keep | 20 | 23 | 22 | $29 |
199 Rockingham Rd. (bet. Rtes. 102 & 111), Derry NH, 603-432-1559
M – The "memories of Robert Frost" and the "pretty setting" are pleasing, more consistently so than the sometimes "disappointing" Continental fare here; though it can be "wonderful", and the service "excellent", too frequently "the food simply doesn't live up to the atmosphere."

Strawbery Court Restaurant Francais* | 22 | 22 | 22 | $30 |
20 Atkinson St. (bet. State & Court Sts.), Portsmouth NH, 603-431-7722
U – This "romantic" Classic French is "worth every penny" of the (for Portsmouth) hefty tab; the "interesting, delicious" fare is the equal of the setting.

WHITE BARN INN | 22 | 25 | 23 | $37 |
White Barn Inn, Beach St. (across from Franciscan Monastery), Kennebunkport ME, 207-967-2321
M – Nearly everyone loves the "picturesque setting" of this little Maine inn, but the cooking is another story; whether the regional cuisine is the "absolute best" or "much ado about nothing" probably has much to do with whether you can tell where the scenery ends and the seasoning begins.

INDEX TO RESTAURANTS

SPECIAL FEATURES AND APPEALS

TYPES OF CUISINE

American (Traditional)

Anthony's Pier 4
Barnacle
Barrett's
Bay Tower Room
Bennigan's
Blacksmith House
Boston Sail Loft
Boylston's
Brandy Pete's
Cafe Rouge
Cambridge Sail Loft
Charley's Saloon
Claddagh
Clarke's
Commonwealth Brewing
Coolidge Cnr. Club.
Copley's
Cricket's
D.R. Brown's
Durgin Park
Eagle Brook Saloon
Elsie's
57 Restaurant
Freestones
Fuddrucker's
Great House, The
Gourmeli's
Hampshire House
Hard Rock Cafe
Houlihan's
J.C. Hillary's Ltd.
Ken's Steak House
Last Hurrah
Locke-Ober Cafe
Marshside
Newbury Steak House
New Yorker Diner
Oasis Cafe
On the Park
Parker's
Pillar House
Pour House
Red Lion
Salty Dog
Sevens, The
Sherborn Inn
Sports Depot, The
Steak/Neighborhood
Stockyard, The
Tam O'Shanter
Ten Huntington
Thornton's
Tim's Tavern
Top of the Hub
Victoria Diner
Victoria Station
Warren Tavern
Winery Restaurant

American (Contemporary)

Arrows
Aujourd'hui
Back Bay Bistro
Bello Mondo
Bennett Street Cafe
Black Forest Cafe
Blue Strawbery
Bluestone Bistro
Blue Wave
Boodle's of Boston
Bristol Lounge
Candleworks
Cape Neddick Inn
Chillingsworth
Clarke Cooke House
Cornucopia
Cranberry Moose, The

Dakota's
Finally Michael's
Flash in the Pan
Galley Restaurant
Hamersley's Bistro
Harvard Street Grill
Harvest
High Brewster
Hungry I
Icarus
Jasper's
J.C. Hillary's Ltd.
Jonah's
Mattapoisett Inn
Mill Falls
Rarities
Regatta of Cotuit
Regatta of Falmouth
Ritz Cafe
Rowes Wharf
Seasons
Second Story
Serendipity III
798 Main
St. Botolph
St. Cloud
Straight Wharf
Summerhouse, The
Topper's
29 Newbury
21 Federal
Union Grill
White Barn Inn
White Rainbow

Armenian

Ararat
Karoun

Bar-B-Q

Barbeques Int'l
Boylston's
Buster's Barbecue
Commonwealth Brewing
East Coast Grill
Jimmy Mac's
Loading Zone
New Bridge Cafe
Porterhouse Cafe
Redbone's
Santarpio's Pizza
Village Smokehouse
Vinny Marino's

Brazilian

Buteco
Cafe Brazil

Cajun

Border Cafe
Cajun Yankee
East Coast Grill

Californian

Blue Wave
Bluestone Bistro
Gill's Grill
Paparazzi

Caribbean

Bennett St. Cafe
East Coast Grill
Green Street Grill
Sibel

Chinese

Ahan-Thai
Aku Aku
Bernard's

Cafe China
Carl's Pagoda
Changsho
Chau Chow
Chef Chang's House
Chef Chow's House
China Gate
Dynasty
Eastern Pier Seafood
Four Seas
Golden Palace
Golden Temple
Great House, The
Ho Yuen Ting
Imperial Tea House
Joyce Chen
Kowloon
Lucky Garden
Mary Chung
Ming Garden
Mister Leung's
Moon Villa
New House of Toy
Noble House
Peking Garden
Sally Ling's
Stars Ocean
Ta Chien
Taiwan Taste
Weylu's
Yangtze River
Yenching Palace

Coffee Shops

Blacksmith House
Cafe Paradiso
Cafe Promenade
Cafe Rouge
Cafe Suisse
Cafe Vittoria
Charlie's Sandwich
Il Dolce Momento

Continental

Alexander's
Another Season
Aujourd'hui
Black Pearl
Bridge Street Cafe
Cafe Escadrille
Cafe Promenade
Cafe Suisse
Charles Restaurant
Cornwall's
Different Drummer
Gourmeli's
Hampshire House
Jonah's
Joseph's Aquarium
Le Grande Cafe
Magic Pan
Medieval Manor
Palmer's
Plaza Dining Room
Ports
Promises To Keep
Ritz Dining Room
Schroeder's
Seaside Restaurant
Top of the Hub
Upstairs at the Pudding

Cuban

La Espanola

Delis

B&D Deli
Elsie's
Rebecca's
Rubin's
S&S Restaurant
Stage Deli

Diners

Blue Diner
Dad's Beantown Diner
Modern Diner
New Yorker Diner
Victoria Diner

Eclectic

Alberta's Cafe
Aujourd'hui
Bello Mondo
Biba
Black Dog Tavern
Blue Diner
Boston Sail Loft
Cafe Fleuri
Cafe Florian
Chez Nous
Cityside
Club Cafe
Division Sixteen
Dockside
Frogg Lane
Galley
Gardner Museum Cafe
Great Stuff
Grendel's Den
Hamersley's Bistro
Harvard Bookstore Cafe
Harvard Gardens
Harvard Street Grill
Houlihan's
Johnny D's
Museum of Fine Arts
Pentimento
Rebecca's
S&S Restaurant
Sunset Grill & Tap
Tapas
TGI Friday's
224 Boston St.
Union Grill
Washington Street Bar
White Horse Tavern

Ethiopian

Addis Red Sea
Ethiopian Restaurant

French Bistro

Brasserie Les Halles
Chez Jean
Le Bellecoeur
Le Petit Auberge
Lucky's
Peacock Restaurant
Pot Au Feu

French Classic

Chanticleer
Clarke Cooke House
Du Barry
La Bellecoeur
La Rivage
Le Bocage
Le Grenier
Le Petit Auberge
L'Espalier
Maison Robert
Pot Au Feu
Strawbery Court
Veronique

French Nouvelle

Aujourd'hui
Chez Nous
Chillingsworth
D'Artagnan
Julien
Le Bocage
L'Espalier
L'Etoile/Charlotte Inn
Regatta of Cotuit
Regatta of Falmouth

German

Jacob Wirth Restaurant
Wursthaus, The

Greek

Acropolis
Alexander's
Averof
Bishop's
Demo's Restaurant

Grills

Blue Wave
Boodle's
Brodie's Cafe
Dakota's
East Coast Grill
Gill's Grill
Grill 23
Hilltop Steak House
Joe's American Bar
Last Hurrah
Lyceum Bar & Grill
Newport Grill
Sculler's Grille

Hamburgers

Bull & Finch Pub
Fuddruckers
Hard Rock Cafe
Houlihan's
Mr. Bartley's
Steak/Neighborhood
Tim's Tavern

Health Food

Five Seasons
Jae's Cafe
Milk Street Cafe
Open Sesame

Hungarian

Cafe Budapest

Indian

Barbeques Int'l
India Pavilion
India Royal
Indian Delight
Kebab-N-Kurry
Oh Calcutta
Shalimar of India
Tandoor House
Taste of India

International

Angel's
Biba
Museum of Fine Arts
Rocco's
Tapas
Union Street Cafe

Irish

Black Rose
Claddagh

Italian (Northern)

Azita
Bello Mondo
Bernardo's
Bnu
Caffe Luna
Capucino's
Carlo Marino's
Ciaobella
Ciro's
Davide
Domenico's
Donatello's
Dom's

Giannino's
Il Capriccio
La Groceria
Lucia's Ristorante
Olives
On the Square
Ottavio's
Paparazzi
Ponte Vecchio
Ristorante Toscano
Rosalie's
Saporito
Sfuzzi
Spaghetti Club, The
Spinnaker Italia
Toscano's
Upstairs at the Pudding
Venetian Gardens
Vin & Eddie's

Italian (Southern)

Anchovies
Cafe Marliave
Cantin Abruzzi
La Summa
Newtowne Grille
Piccolo Venezia
Rita's Place
Saraceno's

Italian
(North and South)

Bel Canto
Bella Napoli
Bertucci's Pizza
Black Goose
Botolph's
Buoniconti's
Cafe Amalfi
Cafe Paradiso
Caffe Lampara
Caffe Vittoria
Cantin Abruzzi
Cantina Italiana
Capucino's
Charles Restaurant
Ciro & Sal's
Daily Catch
Da Natale
Emilio's
European Restaurant
Felicia's
Five North Square
Florence's Restaurant
Galleria Umberto
Giacomo's
Grape Vine
G'Vanni's
Il Giardino Cafe
Joe Tecce's
La Trattoria
L'Osteria
Lucia's Ristorante
Mamma Maria
Marino's
Massimino's
Mateo's
Mother Anna's
Navona
Newport Grill
Newtowne Grille
Nicole
Ottavio's
Pagliuca's Restaurant
Palmer's
Piccola Venezia
Pushcart
Sablone's Veal 'n Vintage
Saporito
Schifino
Sorrento's
Spinnaker Italia
Stellina's
Verona
Via Veneto

Villa Francesca
Vinny Marino's

Italian Nuova Cucina

Al Forno
Black Goose
Bnu
Buoniconti's
Davio's
Mamma Maria
Michela's
On the Square
Stellina's
Upstairs/Pudding

Japanese

Bisuteki
Genji
Goemon
Gyosai
Gyuhama
Hanmiok
Kabuki
Kyoto Japanese Stkhse.
Little Osaka
Matsu-ya
Miyako
Nara Restaurant
Roka
Sakura-bana
Shilla
Shogun
Sushi-naguya
Takeshima
Tatsukichi

Jewish

B&D Deli
Milk Street Cafe*
Rubin's
Stage Deli
(*Kosher)

Korean

Hanmiok
Jae's Cafe
Kabuki
Matsu-ya
Nara Restaurant
New Korea
Seoul House
Shilla

Lebanese

Bishop's
Nadia's Eastern Star

Mexican/Tex-Mex

Acapulco
Boca Grande
Border Cafe
Cantares
Casa Elena
Casa Mexico
Casa Romero
Chili's
Fajita Rita's
Green Street Grill
Las Brisas
Mexican Cuisine
Rudy's Cafe
Sami's 24 Hrs.
Sol Azteca
Zuma Tex-Mex Cafe

Middle Eastern

Ararat
Averof
Bishop's
Cafe Rose
Masada
Nadia's
Sabra
Sami's 24 Hrs.

Skewers, The
Sultan's Kitchen
Vinny Marino's

Pizza

Bel Canto
Bertucci's Pizza
Caserta's Pizza
Circle Pizza
European Restaurant
Galeria Umberto
Santarpio's Pizza

Polynesian

Aku Aku

Portuguese

Casa Portugal
Neighborhood Restaurant
O'Fado
P.A. Seafood
Portugalia
Sunset Cafe

Russian

Troyka
Yelena

Seafood

Anthony's Pier 4
Atlantic Fish Co.
Barnacle
Barrett's
Blue Point Oyster Bar
Callahan's
Cao Palace
Chart House
Chatterley's
Cherrystones
Colorado Public Library
Daily Catch
Dover Sea Grille
Eastern Pier Seafood
Freestones
Giacomo's
Happy Haddock
Hemenway's
Ho Yuen Ting
Jimbo's Fish Shanty
Jimmy's Harborside
Jonah's
Joseph's Aquarium
Landing, The
Legal Sea Foods
Mass Bay Company
Michael's Waterfront
No Name
Ports
Salty Dog
Seaside Restaurant
Skipjack's
Straight Wharf
Turner Fisheries
Union Oyster House
Venus Seafood
Village Fish, The
Willow Pond Kitchen

South American

Cantares
Casa Elena
Los Andes

Southern/Soul

Bob the Chef
Cajun Yankee
Jimmy Mac's
Redbone's

Southwestern

Border Cafe
Cactus Club

Chili's
Cottonwood Cafe
Washington Street Bar
Zuma Tex-Mex Cafe

Spanish

Casa Elena
Dali
Iruna
P.A. Seafood
Sunset Cafe
Tapas

Steak Houses

Bisuteki
Boylston's
Callahan's
Chart House
Colorado Public Library
Dakota's
D.R. Brown's
Grill 23
Hilltop Steak House
Ken's Steak House
Michael's Waterfront
Morton's of Chicago
Newbury Steak House
Steak/Neighborhood
Stockyard, The

Thai

Ahan-Thai
Amarin of Thailand
Amarin II
Bangkok Bistro
Bangkok Cuisine
House of Siam
King & I
Kowloon
Montien
Pattaya
Rama Thai
Sawasdee
Siam Cuisine
Soom Thai
Star of Siam
Thai Cuisine
Thai House
Tien's Thai

Turkish

Sultan's Kitchen

Vegetarian
(Most Chinese, Indian and Thai restaurants and the following)

Five Seasons
Jae's Cafe
Open Sesame
Streets Cafe

Vietnamese

Cao Palace
Pho Pasteur
Viet Restaurant

NEIGHBORHOOD LOCATIONS

Back Bay

Acapulco
Atlantic Fish Co.
Aujourd'hui
Back Bay Bistro
Bello Mondo
Biba
Blue Wave
Boodle's of Boston
Bristol Lounge
Bull & Finch Pub
Cactus Club
Cafe Budapest
Cafe De Paris
Cafe Florian
Cafe Rouge
Casa Romero
Charley's Saloon
Chili's
Ciaobella
Copley's
Dad's Beantown Diner
Davio's
Division Sixteen
Du Barry
Genji
Grill 23
Gyuhama
Hard Rock Cafe
Harvard Bookstore Cafe
House of Siam
J.C. Hillary's Ltd.
Joe's American Bar
Kebab-N-Kurry
King & I
Legal Sea Foods
Le Grand Cafe
L'Espalier
Magic Pan
Mass Bay Company
Mister Leung's
Morton's of Chicago
Newbury Steak House
Paparazzi
Plaza Dining Room
Pour House
Rebecca's
Ritz Cafe
Ritz Dining Room
Skipjack's
Stage Deli
Star of Siam
St. Botolph
Steak/Neighborhood
Streets Cafe
Ten Huntington
TGI Friday's
Top of the Hub
Turner Fisheries
29 Newbury
Yenching Palace

Beacon Hill

Ahan-Thai
Another Season
Bel Canto
Black Goose
Charles Restaurant
Hampshire House
Harvard Gardens
Hungry I
Il Dolce Momento
King & I
La Trattoria
Rebecca's
Ristorante Toscano
Sevens, The

Chinatown

Carl's Pagoda
Chau Chow
China Gate
Dynasty
Four Seas
Golden Palace
Ho Yuen Ting
Imperial Tea House
Moon Villa
New House of Toy
Pho Pasteur
Taiwan Taste
Viet Restaurant

Downtown Boston

Bay Tower Room
Blue Diner
Brandy Pete's
Cafe Fleuri
Cafe Marliave
Cafe Suisse
Commonwealth Brewing
Cornucopia
Dakota's
Fajita Rita's
Julien
Last Hurrah
Loading Zone
Locke-Ober Cafe
Maison Robert
Milk Street Cafe
Nara Restaurant
Parker's
Schifino
Schroeder's
Sultan's Kitchen

Fanueil Hall

Bertucci's Pizza
Black Rose
Brasserie Les Halles
Cityside
Clarke's
Cricket's
Dockside
Durgin Park
Frogg Lane
Great Stuff
Gyosai
Houlihan's
Salty Dog
Seaside Restaurant
Seasons
Serendipity III
Tatsukichi
Zuma Tex-Mex Cafe

Symphony

Bangkok Cuisine
Cafe Promenade
Ethiopian Restaurant
Soom Thai
Thai Cuisine

Theater District

Bennigan's
Bnu
Cafe Rouge
57 Restaurant
Fuddrucker's
Jacob Wirth Restaurant
Joyce Chen
Montien
Pho Pasteur
Rocco's
Stage Deli

Waterfront

Anthony's Pier 4
Boston Sail Loft
Chart House
Chatterley's
Cherrystones

Daily Catch
Eastern Pier Seafood
Jasper's
Jimbo's Fish Shanty
Jimmy's Harborside
Las Brisas
Michael's Waterfront
No Name
Rowes Wharf
Sally Ling's
Venus Seafood
Victoria Station
Weylu's
Winery Restaurant

Kenmore Square/Fenway

Aku Aku
B&D Deli
Buteco
Cornwall's
D.R. Brown's
Gardner Museum Cafe
Il Giardino Cafe
Miyako
Museum Restaurant
Sami's 24 Hrs.
Sibel
Sorrento's
Stars Ocean
Ta Chien

North End

Bella Napoli
Bernardo's
Cafe Paradiso
Caffe Vittoria
Cantina Italiana
Carlo Marino's
Circle Pizza
Daily Catch
Da Natale
Davide
Dom's
Emilio's
European Restaurant
Felicia's
Five North Square
Florence's Restaurant
Galeria Umberto
Giacomo's
G'vanni's
Joe Tecce's
Joseph's Aquarium
La Summa
L'Osteria
Lucia's Ristorante
Mamma Maria
Massimino's
Mateo's
Mother Anna's
Nicole
Oasis Cafe
Ottavio's
Pagliuca's Restaurant
Piccolo Venezia
Pushcart
Saraceno's
Union Oyster House
Via Veneto
Villa Francesca

South End/Roxbury

Addis Red Sea
Anchovies
Azita
Bob the Chef
Botolph's on Tremont
Buteco
Charlie's Sandwich
Claddagh
Club Cafe
Hamersley's Bistro
Icarus
Jae's Cafe & Grill
Medieval Manor
Nadia's Eastern Star

On the Park
St. Botolph
St. Cloud
Thornton's
Tim's Tavern
Victoria Diner

Cambridge – Central Square

Bel Canto
Green Street Grill
India Pavilion
Jonah's
Kabuki
La Groceria
Mary Chung
Sally Ling's
798 Main
Shalimar of India
Spinnaker Italia

Cambridge – Fresh Pond

Aku Aku
Joyce Chen
Little Osaka
Pentimento

Cambridge – Harvard Square

Bel Canto
Bennett Street Cafe
Bertucci's Pizza
Bisuteki
Black Rose
Blacksmith House
Border Cafe
Casa Mexico
Changsho
Chef Chow's House
Chez Jean
Chez Nous
Chili's
Dali
Elsie's
Giannino's
Grendel's Den
Harvest
Iruna
Lucky Garden
Mr. Bartley's
Newtowne Grille
Peacock Restaurant
Rarities
Roka
Sakura-bana
Shilla
Skewers, The
Spaghetti Club, The
Tandoor House
Troyka
Upstairs/Pudding
Wursthaus, The

Cambridge – Inman Square

Cafe China
Cajun Yankee
Cantares
Casa Portugal
East Coast Grill
New Korea
Portugalia
S&S Restaurant
Sunset Cafe

Cambridge – Kendall Square

Bertucci's Pizza
Boca Grande
Cambridge Sail Loft
Buoniconti's
Davio's

Goemon
Legal Sea Foods
Michela's

Cambridge – Porter Square

Acropolis
Averof
Black Forest Cafe
Cottonwood Cafe
Jimmy Mac's
Marino's
Matsu-ya
Mexican Cuisine
Newtowne Grille
Porterhouse Cafe
Tapas

Jamaica Plain/ West Roxbury

Acapulco
Five Seasons
La Espanola
Los Andes
Vinny Marino's

Allston/Brighton

Barbeques Int'l
Bluestone Bistro
Cafe Brazil
Caffe Lampara
Cao Palace
Chef Chow's House
Hanmiok
India Royal
Rama Thai
Sculler's Grille
Siam Cuisine
Sports Depot, The
Stockyard, The
Sunset Grill & Tap

Thai House
Yelena

Chelsea/East Boston

Domenico's
New Bridge Cafe
Rita's Place
Sablone's Veal 'n Vintage
Santarpio's Pizza

Brookline/ Chestnut Hill

Alexander's
B&D Deli
Bangkok Bistro
Bernardo's
Bertucci's Pizza
Boylston's
Caffe Lampara
Caffe Luna
Capucino's
Charley's Saloon
Chef Chang's House
Chef Chow's House
Ciro's
Cityside
Colorado Public Library
Coolidge Cnr. Club.
Davio's
Dover Sea Grille
Golden Temple
Harvard Street Grill
Legal Sea Foods
Masada
Ming Garden
Noble House
Open Sesame
Paparazzi
Pattaya
Rubin's
Sawasdee
Sfuzzi

Skipjack's
Sol Azteca
Stage Deli
Sushi-Nagoya

Takeshima
Village Fish, The
Village Smokehouse

SUBURBS

Charlestown

Barrett's
Olives
Warren Tavern

Lexington/Concord

Bel Canto
China Gate
Willow Pond Kitchen
Yangtze River

Newton/Needham

Amarin
Bertucci's Pizza
Callahan's
Capucino's
Karoun
Mill Falls
Pillar House
Sabra
Sally Ling's
Seoul House
Shogun
Sol Azteca
Union Street Cafe

Somerville/Medford

Bertucci's Pizza
Happy Haddock
Johnny D's
Neighborhood Restaurant
P.A. Seafood
Redbones
Rudy's Cafe

Watertown/Waltham

Amarin (Wellesley)
Ararat
Cafe Rose
Casa Elena
Demo's Restaurant
Il Capriccio
Le Bocage
New Yorker Diner
On the Square
Stellina's
Taste of India
Verona

OUTLYING SUBURBS

North of Boston

Barnacle
Bertucci's Pizza
Bishop's
Border Cafe
Brodie's Cafe
Cafe Escadrille
Capucino's
Charley's Saloon
Donatello's
Flash in the Pan
Grape Vine
Hilltop Steak House
Kowloon
Landing, The
Lucia's Ristorante

Lyceum Bar & Grill
O'Fado
Palmer's
Ponte Vecchio
Rosalie's
Tien's Thai
Union Grill
Washington Street Bar
Weylu's
White Rainbow

West of Boston

Amarin II
Bel Canto
Bertucci's Pizza
Charley's Saloon
Finally Michael's
Gill's Grill
Il Capriccio
Ken's Steak House

Le Bellecoeur
Legal Sea Foods
Oh Calcutta
Ports
Sherborn Inn

South of Boston

Bertucci's Pizza
Bridge Street Cafe
Candleworks
Eagle Brook Saloon
Freestones
J.C. Hillary's Ltd.
La Rivage
Mattapoisett Inn
Navona
Red Lion
Saporito
Vin & Eddie's
Weylu's

FAR OUTLYING AREAS

Cape Cod

Chillingsworth
Ciro & Sal's
Cranberry Moose
High Brewster
Marshside
Regatta of Cotuit
Regatta of Falmouth

Maine

Alberta's Cafe
Arrows
Cape Neddick Inn
White Barn Inn

Martha's Vineyard

Black Dog Tavern
Le Grenier
L'Etoile

Nantucket

Chanticleer
Galley Restaurant
Second Story
Straight Wharf
Summerhouse, The
Topper's
21 Federal

New Hampshire

Blue Strawbery
D'Artagnan
Promises To Keep
Strawbery Court

Rhode Island

Al Forno
Angel's
Black Pearl
Blue Point Oyster Bar
Caserta's Pizza
Clarke Cooke House
Great House, The
Hemenway's
Le Petit Auberge
Lucky's
Modern Diner
Newport Grill
Pot Au Feu
Toscano's
White Horse Tavern

SPECIAL FEATURES AND APPEALS

Bar Scenes

Aku Aku
Bennigan's
Border Cafe
Boston Sail Loft
Botolph's on Tremont
Cactus Club
Cafe Escadrille
Caffe Vittoria
Charley's Saloon
Chatterley's
Cityside
Clarke's
Club Cafe
Commonwealth Brewing
Coolidge Cnr. Club.
Cottonwood Cafe
Cricket's
Dakota's
Dali
Davio's
Division Sixteen
Eagle Brook Saloon
Gill's Grill
Hard Rock Cafe
Icarus
Joe's American Bar
Landing, The
Las Brisas
Last Hurrah
Loading Zone
Lyceum Bar & Grill
Michela's
Porterhouse Cafe
Pour House
Rocco's
Rudy's Cafe
Sculler's Grille
Seaside Restaurant
Sevens, The
Sfuzzi
Spaghetti Club, The
Sports Depot, The
St. Botolph
St. Cloud
Steak/Neighborhood
Sunset Grill & Tap
Tam O'Shanter, The
TGI Friday's
29 Newbury
21 Federal
Via Veneto
Vin & Eddie's
Warren Tavern
Washington Street Bar
Winery Restaurant

Breakfast
(All major hotels and the following standouts)

B&D Deli
Bennett Street Cafe
Black Dog Tavern
Blacksmith House
Blue Diner
Bob the Chef
Boodle's of Boston
Brandy Pete's
Cafe Fleuri
Cafe Florian
Cafe Promenade
Cafe Rouge
Cafe Suisse
Charlie's Sandwich
Dad's Beantown Diner
Fuddrucker's
Harvard Bookstore Cafe
Il Dolce Momento
Il Giardino Cafe
Marshside

Milk Street Cafe
Modern Diner
Mr. Bartley's
Neighborhood Restaurant
New Yorker Diner
Open Sesame
Parker's
Pentimento
Pho Pasteur
Pour House
Rebecca's
Ritz Cafe
Rowes Wharf
S&S Restaurant
Seasons
Stage Deli
Streets Cafe
Thornton's
Wursthaus, The

Business Dining

Anthony's Pier 4
Aujourd'hui
Bay Tower Room
Bello Mondo
Bennett Street Cafe
Bisuteki
Brandy Pete's
Bristol Lounge
Cafe Escadrille
Cafe Fleuri
Cafe Marliave
Cafe Promenade
Cornucopia
Dakota's
57 Restaurant
Gill's Grill
Grill 23
Gyuhama
Julien
Kowloon
Locke-Ober Cafe
Maison Robert
Mass Bay Company

Michela's
Mill Falls
Mister Leung's
Montien
Morton's of Chicago
On the Square
Parker's
Pillar House
Ports
Pot Au Feu
Rarities
Ritz Cafe
Ritz Dining Room
Rocco's
Rowes Wharf
Sakura-bana
Schroeder's
Seasons
St. Cloud
Ten Huntington
Toscano's
Via Veneto

BYO Wine or Beer

Black Dog Tavern
Boca Grande
Cafe Rose
Cao Palace
Casa Mexico
Ethiopian Restaurant
Hanmiok
Il Dolce Momento
Le Grenier
Little Osaka
Mary Chung
Moon Villa
Neighborhood Restaurant
Open Sesame
Seoul House
Skewers, The
Taiwan Taste
Troyka

Caters
(Some of the many, in addition to hotel restaurants)

Aku Aku
Alexander's
Another Season
B&D Deli
Black Forest Cafe
Black Goose
Buster's Barbecue
Cactus Club
Chillingsworth
Club Cafe
Cornucopia
East Coast Grill
Green Street Grill
Grill 23
Harvest
High Brewster
Joyce Chen
La Groceria
Le Bocage
Legal Sea Foods
Le Grand Cafe
Locke-Ober Cafe
Lucia's Ristorante
Maison Robert
Massimino's
Michela's
Milk Street Cafe
Mister Leung's
Olives
On the Square
Pagliuca's Restaurant
Rebecca's
Redbones
Rubin's
Sally Ling's
S&S Restaurant
Skipjack's
Stage Deli
St. Botolph
St. Cloud
Sultan's Kitchen
Tatsukichi
29 Newbury
Venus Seafood
Via Veneto
Village Fish, The
Village Smokehouse
Zuma Tex-Mex Cafe

Dancing
(Nightclubs and the following; check times)

Bay Tower Room
Bello Mondo
Buster's Barbecue
Cafe Escadrille
Cantares
Claddagh
Clarke Cooke House
Houlihan's
Karoun
Kowloon
Las Brisas
Last Hurrah
Spaghetti Club, The
Tam O'Shanter, The
Top of the Hub
Union Street Cafe
Weylu's
Winery Restaurant
Yelena

Delivers
(Almost all Chinese, delis and pizzerias deliver; here are some good additional bets; call to check range and charges, if any)

Acapulco
Aku Aku
Bangkok Bistro
Black Goose

Blue Wave
Bluestone Bistro
Buoniconti's
Cafe Rose
Capucino's
Charley's Saloon
Davio's
Division Sixteen
Dom's
Ethiopian Restaurant
Freestones
Great Stuff
G'vanni's
Harvard Bookstore Cafe
India Pavilion
J.C. Hillary's Ltd.
Jimmy Mac's
Joe's American Bar
Karoun
Kebab-N-Kurry
La Espanola
La Groceria
Legal Sea Foods
Masada
Matsu-ya
Mattapoisett Inn
Milk Street Cafe
Mill Falls
Oasis Cafe
Open Sesame
Paparazzi
Parker's
Pho Pasteur
Rebecca's
Redbones
Roka
Sabra
Sakura-bana
Seoul House
Skipjack's
Sorrento's
Steak/Neighborhood
Sultan's Kitchen

Sunset Grill & Tap
Thai Cuisine
Vinny Marino's
Yelena

Dessert (D) and Ice Cream (I)
(Besides Ben & Jerry's, Haagen-Dazs, Herrell's and Steve's)

Bennigan's (D)
Black Forest Cafe (D)
Cafe De Paris (I)
Cafe Paradiso (D,I)
Caffe Vittoria (I)
Capucino's (D)
Chillingsworth (D)
Copley's (D)
Davio's (D)
Frogg Lane (D)
Fuddrucker's (D)
Giannino's (D)
Gill's Grill (D)
Grape Vine (D)
Hard Rock Cafe (D)
Harvard Street Grill (D)
Harvest (D)
Houlihan's (D)
Il Dolce Momento (I)
La Groceria (D)
Le Grand Cafe (D)
Magic Pan (D)
Museum Restaurant (D)
Neighborhood Rest. (D)
On the Park (D)
Pentimento (D)
Rebecca's (D)
Serendipity III (I)
Sfuzzi (D)
Stage Deli (D)
St. Cloud (D)
Steak/Neighborhood (D)
Tam O'Shanter, The (D)

TGI Friday's (D)
Thornton's (D)
29 Newbury (D)
Union Grill (D)
Union Street Cafe (D)

Rowes Wharf
Skipjack's
Sorrento's
Stage Deli
St. Cloud
Turner Fisheries

Dining Alone
(Other than hotels, sushi bars and places with counter service)

Another Season
Aujourd'hui
B&D Deli
Bennett Street Cafe
Black Forest Cafe
Blacksmith House
Blue Diner
Bluestone Bistro
Bristol Lounge
Cafe De Paris
Cafe Fleuri
Cafe Promenade
Cafe Suisse
Caffe Vittoria
Charlie's Sandwich
Gardner Museum Cafe
Goemon
Harvard Bookstore Cafe
Julien
La Groceria
Maison Robert
Museum Restaurant
On the Park
On the Square
Open Sesame
Pattaya
Pentimento
Piccolo Venezia
Plaza Dining Room
Rebecca's
Ristorante Toscano
Ritz Cafe
Ritz Dining Room

Entertainment
(Check times)

Aku Aku (comedy)
Alexander's (jazz)
Aujourd'hui (piano/bass)
Averof (belly dancing)
B&D Deli (Boston)(bands)
Bay Tower Room (piano)
Bishop's (belly dancing)
Bnu (jazz trio)
Brandy Pete's (piano, bands)
Bristol Lounge (piano)
Buster's Barbecue (rock and roll)
Buteco (guitarist)
Cafe Escadrille (jazz)
Cantares (band)
Clarke Cooke House (band)
Club Cafe (piano & singer)
Commonwealth Brewing (reggae)
Cricket's (jazz piano)
57 Restaurant (piano)
Green Street Grill (jazz - blues)
Hampshire House (piano-bass sing-along)
Hampshire House (piano)
Icarus (Fri. jazz trio)
Johnny D's (jazz)
Jonah's (jazz piano trio)
Julien (piano)
Kowloon (bands/comedy)
Landing, The (guitar)
Las Brisas (trio)

Last Hurrah (swing orchestra)
Lyceum Bar (piano)
Mattapoisett Inn (piano/comedy)
Medieval Manor (theater)
Mill Falls (piano)
Newport Grille (jazz)
Parker's (piano)
Plaza Dining Rm. (piano)
Promises To Keep (piano)
Rarities (piano)
Ritz Dining Room (pianist)
Sculler's Grille (jazz)
Seaside Restaurant (jazz/rock/pop)
Serendipity III (jazz)
Sibel (steel drums)
Skipjack's (Sunday jazz)
Sunset Cafe (violin-guitar)
Tam O'Shanter (band)
Top of the Hub (piano)
Turner Fisheries (jazz)
224 Boston St. (piano)
Union Street Cafe (bands)
Vin & Eddie's (piano)
Vinny Marino's (wkend. dj)
Warren Tavern (r&b)
White Barn Inn (pianist)
Winery Restaurant (jazz)

Fireplaces

Ahan-Thai
Al Forno
B&D Deli (Boston)
Black Dog Tavern
Blacksmith House
Bristol Lounge
Cactus Club
Cafe Brazil
Casa Portugal
Casa Romero
Chanticleer
Chillingsworth
Ciro & Sal's
Clarke Cooke House
Copley's
Cornucopia
D'Artagnan
Donatello's
Dover Sea Grille
Finally Michael's
Freestones
Great House, The
Grendel's Den
Hampshire House
High Brewster
Hungry I
Le Petit Auberge
Locke-Ober Cafe
Lucky's
Lyceum Bar & Grill
Mattapoisett Inn
Navona
Pillar House
Portugalia
Red Lion
Regatta of Cotuit
Schroeder's
Second Story
Stockyard, The
Strawbery Court
21 Federal
Upstairs/Pudding
Warren Tavern
White Barn Inn
White Horse Tavern
White Rainbow

Game in Season

Alberta's Cafe
Al Forno
Angel's
Another Season

- Arrows
- Bay Tower Room
- Biba
- Black Dog Tavern
- Black Goose
- Black Pearl
- Blue Strawbery
- Bridge Street Cafe
- Bristol Lounge
- Cafe Budapest
- Cafe Escadrille
- Cafe Suisse
- Chanticleer
- Chez Jean
- Chillingsworth
- Ciaobella
- Clarke Cooke House
- Club Cafe
- Colorado Public Library
- Cornucopia
- Cornwall's
- Cranberry Moose
- Dakota's
- Dali
- D'Artagnan
- Davide
- Davio's
- Dom's
- Grill 23
- Hamersley's Bistro
- Hampshire House
- Harvard Street Grill
- Harvest
- High Brewster
- Hungry I
- Icarus
- Iruna
- Jasper's
- Le Bocage
- Le Grenier
- Le Petit Auberge
- L'Etoile
- Loading Zone
- Locke-Ober Cafe
- Lucky's
- Maison Robert
- Mamma Maria
- Michael's Waterfront
- Michela's
- Mill Falls
- Navona
- Nicole
- Olives
- On the Square
- Ottavio's
- Parker's
- Peacock Restaurant
- Pillar House
- Porterhouse Cafe
- Ports
- Pot Au Feu
- Promises To Keep
- Rarities
- Rebecca's
- Red Lion
- Ristorante Toscano
- Ritz Dining Room
- Rocco's
- Rowes Wharf
- Seasons
- Second Story
- 798 Main
- Sfuzzi
- St. Botolph
- St. Cloud
- Strawbery Court
- Ten Huntington
- 29 Newbury
- 21 Federal
- 224 Boston St.
- Union Grill
- Upstairs/Pudding
- White Barn Inn
- White Horse Tavern

Garden/Outdoor Dining

Alexander's
Atlantic Fish Co.
Back Bay Bistro
Barnacle
Bel Canto
Bennett Street Cafe
Bertucci's Pizza
Black Dog Tavern
Black Goose
Black Pearl
Blacksmith House
Blue Point Oyster Bar
Bnu
Boston Sail Loft
Brandy Pete's
Bridge Street Cafe
Cactus Club
Cafe Florian
Cafe Marliave
Cambridge Sail Loft
Chanticleer
Charley's Saloon
Chatterley'
Cherrystones
Ciaobella
Cityside
Clarke Cooke House
Cricket's
Du Barry
Eagle Brook Saloon
Galley Restaurant
Gardner Museum Cafe
Giannino's
Grape Vine
Harvard Bookstore Cafe
Harvest
Hemenway's
Hungry I
Iruna
Joe's American Bar
Landing, The
La Rivage
Le Grand Cafe
Le Grenier
Le Petit Auberge
L'Etoile
Magic Pan
Maison Robert
Mattapoisett Inn
Michael's Waterfront
Milk Street Cafe
Mill Falls
Museum Restaurant
Neighborhood Restaurant
Ottavio's
Promises To Keep
Salty Dog
Sami's 24 Hrs.
Seaside Restaurant
Serendipity III
Skipjack's
Stellina's
Straight Wharf
Thornton's
29 Newbury
224 Boston St.
Union Grill
Union Street Cafe
Venus Seafood
Victoria Station
Winery Restaurant
Yelena

Happy Hour

Brandy Pete's
Buster's Barbecue
Cantares
Charley's Saloon
Club Cafe
Genji
Grendel's Den
Jacob Wirth Restaurant
J.C. Hillary's Ltd.

Jimmy's Harborside
Joe's American Bar
Jonah's
Las Brisas
Last Hurrah
Le Petit Auberge
Locke-Ober Cafe
Maison Robert
Michael's Waterfront
Parker's
Schroeder's
Sculler's Grille
Serendipity III
Sfuzzi
Spinnaker Italia
Sunset Grill & Tap
TGI Friday's
224 Boston St.
Warren Tavern

Health/Spa Menus

Atlantic Fish Co.
Bello Mondo
Bennett Street Cafe
Bennigan's
Border Cafe
Brandy Pete's
Bristol Lounge
Cactus Club
Cafe Brazil
Cafe Fleuri
Cafe Florian
Cafe Rouge
Cafe Suisse
Cape Neddick Inn
Chili's
Clarke Cooke House
Club Cafe
Colorado Public Library
Cricket's
Dakota's
Dover Sea Grille
Five Seasons
Hampshire House
Happy Haddock
Harvard Bookstore Cafe
Hemenway's
Jae's Cafe
Jonah's
Kowloon
La Espanola
Last Hurrah
Legal Sea Foods
Loading Zone
Matsu-ya
Mill Falls
Museum Restaurant
Olives
Open Sesame
Parker's
Rarities
Ritz Cafe
Ritz Dining Room
Rocco's
Sabra
Sculler's Grille
Seasons
Second Story
Skipjack's
Streets Cafe
TGI Friday's
Top of the Hub
Union Grill
Upstairs/Pudding
Venetian Garden
Venus Seafood
Yangtze River

Historic Interest

Arrows
Black Pearl
Blacksmith House
Blue Strawbery
Boston Sail Loft

Cafe Marliave
Cantina Italiana
Chillingsworth
Ciro & Sal's
Cranberry Moose
D'Artagnan
Durgin Park
High Brewster
Jacob Wirth Restaurant
Le Petit Auberge
Locke-Ober Cafe
Maison Robert
Mill Falls
Nara Restaurant
Pot Au Feu
Red Lion
Regatta of Cotuit
Schroeder's
21 Federal
Union Oyster House
Upstairs/Pudding
Warren Tavern
White Horse Tavern
Wursthaus, The

Hotel Dining

Back Bay Hilton
  Boodle's of Boston
Boston Harbor Hotel
  Rowes Wharf
Bostonian Hotel
  Seasons
Charles Hotel
  Bennett Street Cafe
  Rarities
Charlotte Inn (Martha's Vineyard)
  L'Etoile
Colonnade
  Cafe Promenade
Copley Hotel
  Cafe Budapest
Copley Plaza
  Copley's
  Plaza Dining Room
Embassy Suites Hotel
  Sculler's Grille
Four Seasons
  Aujourd'hui
  Bristol Lounge
Hotel Lafayette
  Le Marquis de Lafayette
  Cafe Suisse
Hotel Sonesta
  Davio's
Howard Johnson's (Camb.)
  Bisuteki
Howard Johnson's Hotel
  57 Restaurant
Hyatt Cambridge
  Jonah's
  Sally Ling's
  Spinnaker Italia
Lafayette
  Cafe Suisse
Marriott Copley Plaza
  Bello Mondo
  Gourmeli's
Marriott Long Wharf
  Chatterley's
Meridien Hotel
  Cafe Fleuri
  Julien
Omni Parker House
  Last Hurrah
  Parker's
Park Plaza Hotel
  Cafe Rouge
  Legal Sea Foods
Ritz-Carlton Hotel
  Ritz Cafe
  Ritz Dining Room
Sheraton Boston Hotel
  Mass Bay Company
  Steak/Neighborhood

Sherborn Inn
　Sherborn Inn
Vista Hilton
　Ports
Wauwinet Inn (Nantucket)
　Topper's
Westin Hotel
　Ten Huntington
　Turner Fisheries

"In" Places

Al Forno
Biba
Black Pearl
Blue Diner
Blue Point Oyster Bar
Border Cafe
Boston Sail Loft
Botolph's on Tremont
Cactus Club
Cambridge Sail Loft
Chanticleer
Charley's Saloon
Chillingsworth
Ciaobella
Club Cafe
Cottonwood Cafe
Dakota's
Dali
Davio's
Division Sixteen
East Coast Grill
Grill 23
Hamersley's Bistro
Hard Rock Cafe
Harvest
Jasper's
Joe's American Bar
Julien
Landing, The
Loading Zone
Locke-Ober Cafe
Lucky's
Lyceum Bar & Grill
Michela's
Mister Leung's
Morton's of Chicago
Olives
Paparazzi
Pot Au Feu
Rebecca's (Charles St.)
Ritz Cafe
Ritz Dining Room
Rocco's
Rosalie's
Seasons
Second Story
Sfuzzi
St. Cloud
Straight Wharf
21 Federal
224 Boston St.
Warren Tavern
Washington Street Bar

Jacket/Tie Required

Anthony's Pier 4
Aujourd'hui
Bay Tower Room
Cafe Budapest
Chanticleer
Charles Restaurant
Chillingsworth
Davide
57 Restaurant
Hampshire House
L'Espalier
L'Etoile
Locke-Ober Cafe
Maison Robert
Parker's
Pillar House
Plaza Dining Room
Ports
Ritz Cafe
Ritz Dining Room
Rowes Wharf
Sally Ling's

Toscano's
White Barn Inn
White Horse Tavern

Late Dining – After 11 PM

Aku Aku (1)
Anchovies (1)
B&D Deli (2)
Bennigan's (12:30)
Black Pearl (1)
Botolph's (11:30)
Bristol Lounge (11:30)
Cafe Escadrille (12)
Caffe Vittoria (12)
Capucino's (12)
Carl's Pagoda (12)
Casa Portugal (11:30)
Charley's Saloon (12)
Chau Chow (2)
Club Cafe (1)
Coolidge Cnr. Club. (1:15)
Cornwall's (1)
Division Sixteen (1:30)
Domenico's (1)
Eagle Brook Sal. (12)
European (12)
Golden Temple (12:30)
G'vanni's (1)
Gyuhama (2)
Hard Rock Cafe (1)
Il Dolce Momento (12)
Imperial Tea House (2)
J.C. Hillary's Ltd. (12)
Jonah's (11:30)
Kowloon (1:30)
Moon Villa (4)
Nadia's (12:30)
Navona (12)
New Yorker Diner (4)
Olives (11:30)
Paparazzi (1:30)
Pour House (12)
Ritz Cafe (12)
Sami's (24 hrs)
Santarpio's Pizza (12:30)
Sorrento's (12)
Sports Depot, The (12:30)
Stars Ocean (12)
St. Botolph (12)
St. Cloud (12)
Sunset Grill & Tap (1)
Tapas (12:15 AM)
TGI Friday's (12)
Turner Fisheries (11)
Victoria Diner (12)
Weylu's (12)

Noteworthy Newcomers (22)

Alexander's
Anchovies
Azita
Bertucci's Pizza
Blue Wave
Botolph's on Tremont
Buoniconti's
Buster's Barbecue
Caffe Lampara
Charley's Saloon
  (Newbury St.)
Eastern Pier Seafood
Jae's Cafe & Grill
La Espanola
Loading Zone
Marino's
Massimino's
Newport Grille
Paparazzi (Chestnut Hill)
Sibel
Taiwan Taste
Veronique
Yelena

Offbeat

Addis Red Sea
Ararat

Averof
Bangkok Cuisine
Barbeques Int'l
Black Rose
Blue Diner
Bob the Chef
Buteco
Cajun Yankee
Cantares
Cao Palace
Carl's Pagoda
Casa Elena
Casa Portugal
Charlie's Sandwich
Club Cafe
Commonwealth Brewing
Coolidge Cnr. Club.
Dad's Beantown Diner
Daily Catch
Dali
Division Sixteen
Eagle Brook Saloon
East Coast Grill
Elsie's
Ethiopian Restaurant
Flash in the Pan
Green Street Grill
Jimmy Mac's
Johnny D's
La Espanola
Loading Zone
Los Andes
Mary Chung
Medieval Manor
Mexican Cuisine
Modern Diner
Mr. Bartley's
Nadia's Eastern Star
Neighborhood Restaurant
New Bridge Cafe
New Yorker Diner
No Name
Oasis Cafe
On the Park
Open Sesame
Pentimento
Pho Pasteur
Porterhouse Cafe
Pour House
Redbones
Rita's Place
Rocco's
Rudy's Cafe
Santarpio's Pizza
Sevens, The
Sultan's Kitchen
Sunset Cafe
Sunset Grill & Tap
Tam O'Shanter, The
Tim's Tavern
Troyka
Venus Seafood
Victoria Diner
Weylu's
Yelena

Parking/Valet

Atlantic Fish Co.
Aujourd'hui
Biba
Blue Wave
Boylston's
Bristol Lounge
Cactus Club
Cafe Budapest
Cantina Italiana
Charles Restaurant
Charley's Saloon
Chart House
Ciaobella
Cranberry Moose
Dakota's
Da Natale
Davide
Davio's
Golden Temple
Grill 23
Hamersley's Bistro
Hampshire House

Icarus
Jasper's
J.C. Hillary's Ltd.
Jimbo's Fish Shanty
Joe's American Bar
Joseph's Aquarium
Last Hurrah
L'Espalier
Locke-Ober Cafe
Lucia's Ristorante
Maison Robert
Mamma Maria
Michael's Waterfront
Mill Falls
Mister Leung's
Morton's of Chicago
Nara Restaurant
Ottavio's
Paparazzi
Parker's
Plaza Dining Room
Ristorante Toscano
Ritz Cafe
Ritz Dining Room
Rocco's
Rowes Wharf
Sally Ling's
Schroeder's
Seasons
Sfuzzi
St. Botolph
St. Cloud
Stockyard, The
Ten Huntington
Via Veneto

Parties
(Any nightclub at off-hours; see also Private Rooms and the following)

Acropolis
Ahan-Thai
Aku Aku
Alexander's
Another Season
Arrows
Aujourd'hui
Averof
B&D Deli
Barrett's
Bay Tower Room
Bel Canto
Bernardo's
Bishop's
Black Dog Tavern
Black Pearl
Black Rose
Blue Strawbery
Blue Wave
Bob the Chef
Boodle's of Boston
Brandy Pete's
Buoniconti's
Buster's Barbecue
Cactus Club
Cafe Amalfi
Cafe Budapest
Cafe Escadrille
Caffe Lampara
Callahan's
Candleworks
Cantares
Cantina Italiana
Capucino's
Charley's Saloon
Chart House
Cherrystones
Chez Jean
Chillingsworth
Ciro & Sal's
Clarke Cooke House
Club Cafe
Colorado Public Lib.
Commonwealth Brew.
Copley's

Cornucopia
Cottonwood Cafe
Cranberry Moose
Cricket's
Dakota's
Dali
D'Artagnan
Davide
Davio's
Domenico's
Dom's
Donatello's
Du Barry
Dynasty
Eagle Brook Saloon
European Restaurant
Felicia's
57 Restaurant
Finally Michael's
Freestones
Frogg Lane
Genji
Gill's Grill
Golden Palace
Golden Temple
Great House, The
Grill 23
G'vanni's
Gyuhama
Hampshire House
Happy Haddock
Hard Rock Cafe
Harvard Gardens
Harvest
Hemenway's
High Brewster
Hilltop Stkhse.
Houlihan's
Hungry I
Icarus
Il Giardino Cafe
India Pavilion
Iruna

Jimmy's
Joe Tecce's
Jonah's
Joseph's Aquarium
Joyce Chen
Ken's Steak House
King & I
Kowloon
Kowloon
La Espanola
Landing, The
Las Brisas
Last Hurrah
La Summa
Le Bellecoeur
Le Bocage
Le Grand Cafe
Le Petit Auberge
L'Espalier
Loading Zone
Locke-Ober Cafe
Lucia's Ristorante
Lyceum Bar & Grill
Magic Pan
Maison Robert
Mamma Maria
Massimino's
Mattapoisett Inn
Medieval Manor
Michael's
Michela's
Mill Falls
Mister Leung's
Modern Diner
Mother Anna's
Museum Restaurant
Nara Restaurant
Navona
New Bridge Cafe
Newbury Stkhse.
New House of Toy
New Korea
Newport Grille

Nicole	Spaghetti Club, The
Noble House	Spinnaker Italia
Oasis Cafe	Stage Deli
Olives	Stars Ocean
On the Park	St. Botolph
On the Square	Stellina's
Open Sesame	Strawbery Court
Ottavio's	Streets Cafe
Palmer's	Sultan's Kitchen
Parker's	Sunset Grill & Tap
Peking Garden	Ta Chien
Pillar House	Takeshima
Portugalia	Tam O'Shanter
Pot Au Feu	Tapas
Promises To Keep	Taste of India
Pushcart	Tatsukichi
Rarities	Ten Huntington
Red Lion	Thornton's
Regatta of Cotuit	Tien's Thai
Regatta/Falmouth	Top of the Hub
Ristorante Toscano	Toscano's
Rita's Place	Turner Fisheries
Ritz Dining Room	29 Newbury
Rocco's	224 Boston St.
Rosalie's	Union Grill
Rowes Wharf	Union Oyster Hse.
Sabra	Union Street Cafe
Sally Ling's	Upstairs/Pudding
Salty Dog	Venetian Garden
S&S Restaurant	Venus Seafood
Sawasdee	Via Veneto
Schroeder's	Victoria Diner
Seaside	Victoria Station
Seasons	Viet Restaurant
Second Story	Villa Francesca
Serendipity III	Village Fish, The
Sfuzzi	Village Smokehouse
Sherborn Inn	Vin & Eddie's
Siam Cuisine	Vinny Marino's
Sibel	Warren Tavern
Skewers, The	Weylu's
Skipjack's	White Barn Inn
Sol Azteca	White Horse Tavern

Winery
Wursthaus, The
Yangtze River
Yelena
Yenching Palace

Private Rooms
(All major hotels, plus the following)

Aku Aku
Alexander's
Another Season
Arrows
Aujourd'hui
Averof
Back Bay Bistro
B&D Deli
Barrett's
Bay Tower Room
Bel Canto
Bernardo's
Bishop's
Black Pearl
Black Rose
Blue Strawbery
Blue Wave
Bob the Chef
Boodle's of Boston
Boston Sail Loft
Boylston's
Brandy Pete's
Buoniconti's
Buster's BBQ
Cafe Amalfi
Cafe Budapest
Cafe Escadrille
Caffe Lampara
Callahan's
Candleworks
Cantina Italiana
Capucino's
Charley's Saloon
Chart House
Cherrystones
Chez Jean
Chillingsworth
Claddagh
Clarke Cooke House
Club Cafe
Colorado Public Library
Commonwealth Brew.
Copley's
Cornucopia
Cranberry Moose
Cricket's
Dakota's
Dali
Davide
Davio's
Dockside
Dom's
Donatello's
Du Barry
Dynasty
Eagle Brook Saloon
European Restaurant
Felicia's
57 Restaurant
Finally Michael's
Frogg Lane
Genji
Gill's Grill
Golden Palace
Golden Temple
Great House, The
Gyosai
Gyuhama
Hampshire House
Happy Haddock
Hard Rock Cafe
Harvest
Hemenway's
High Brewster
Hilltop Steak House
Houlihan's
Iruna

Jimmy's Harborside
Joe Tecce's
Jonah's
Joseph's Aquarium
Joyce Chen
Ken's Steak House
King & I
Kowloon
Las Brisas
Last Hurrah
La Summa
Le Bocage
Le Grand Cafe
Le Petit Auberge
Loading Zone
Locke-Ober Cafe
Lucia's Ristorante
Lyceum Bar & Grill
Magic Pan
Maison Robert
Mamma Maria
Massimino's
Mattapoisett Inn
Michela's
Mill Falls
Mister Leung's
Modern Diner
Mother Anna's
Museum Rest.
Nara Restaurant
Navona
Newport Grille
Nicole
Noble House
No Name
On the Square
Ottavio's
Parker's
Peking Garden
Pillar House
Ports
Promises To Keep
Pushcart

Rarities
Regatta of Cotuit
Regatta of Falmouth
Ristorante Toscano
Rita's Place
Ritz Dining Room
Rocco's
Rosalie's
Rowes Wharf
Sabra
Sally Ling's
S&S Restaurant
Schroeder's
Seasons
Second Story
Serendipity III
Sherborn Inn
Siam Cuisine
Sibel
Skipjack's
St. Botolph
Stellina's
Stockyard, The
Strawbery Court
Sultan's Kitchen
Sunset Grill & Tap
Ta Chien
Tapas
Tatsukichi
Ten Huntington
Tien's Thai
Top of the Hub
Toscano's
224 Boston St.
Union Oyster House
Union Street Cafe
Upstairs/Pudding
Via Veneto
Victoria Diner
Victoria Station
Villa Francesca
Village Smokehouse
Vin & Eddie's

Vinny Marino's
Warren Tavern
Weylu's
White Barn Inn
White Horse Tavern
Winery Restaurant
Wursthaus, The
Yangtze River

People-Watching

B&D Deli
Biba
Black Pearl
Blacksmith House
Bristol Lounge
Cactus Club
Cafe Florian
Cafe Paradiso
Cityside
Club Cafe
Cricket's
Elsie's
Frogg Lane
Giannino's
Grill 23
Harvard Bookstore Cafe
Harvest
Joe's American Bar
Magic Pan
Michela's
Paparazzi
Ritz Cafe
Ritz Dining Room
Rocco's
Rowes Wharf
Salty Dog
Serendipity III
St. Cloud
Thornton's
29 Newbury

Power Scenes

Al Forno
Another Season
Aujourd'hui
Bay Tower Room
Biba
Cafe Budapest
Chanticleer
Chillingsworth
Dakota's
Grill 23
Harvest
Jasper's
Julien
L'Espalier
Locke-Ober Cafe
Lucky's
Maison Robert
Michela's
Mister Leung's
Olives
Parker's
Plaza Dining Room
Rarities
Ritz Cafe
Ritz Dining Room
Rowes Wharf
Seasons
St. Cloud

Pre-Theater/ Early-Bird Menus

Aujourd'hui
Barrett's
Bernardo's
Bnu
Boylston's
Chart House
Cherrystones
Chez Nous
Dover Sea Grille
Jonah's
Mill Falls

Sculler's Grille
Union Street Cafe
Warren Tavern

Post-Theater/Prix-Fixe Menus
(Call to check prices and times)

Alberta's Cafe
B&D Deli
Boylston's
Buster's Barbecue
Cafe Florian
Capucino's
Charley's Saloon
Cherrystones
Claddagh
Cottonwood Cafe
Davide
57 Restaurant
Freestones
Genji
Happy Haddock
Hard Rock Cafe
Jimbo's Fish Shanty
Joseph's Aquarium
Last Hurrah
La Trattoria
Le Petit Auberge
Mill Falls
Portugalia
Ritz Cafe
Sabra
Sunset Cafe
Ten Huntington
Victoria Diner
Warren Tavern

Reservations Essential

Amarin II
Biba
Blue Strawbery
Bnu
Boston Sail Loft
Chanticleer
Charles Restaurant
Chef Chow's House
Cherrystones
Chillingsworth
Ciaobella
Ciro & Sal's
Ciro's
Cranberry Moose
D'Artagnan
Davide
Emilio's
Finally Michael's
Flash in the Pan
Gill's Grill
Goemon
Grape Vine
Hamersley's Bistro
Harvard Street Grill
High Brewster
Icarus
Landing, The
Le Grenier
L'Espalier
L'Etoile
Locke-Ober Cafe
Lyceum Bar & Grill
Medieval Manor
Michael's Waterfront
Museum Restaurant
O'Fado
Ottavio's
Palmer's
Paparazzi
Peacock Restaurant
Pillar House
Plaza Dining Room
Ports
Pot Au Feu
Rarities

Ristorante Toscano
Ritz Dining Room
Rosalie's
Sally Ling's
Seasons
Sfuzzi
Sherborn Inn
Spinnaker Italia
Straight Wharf
Tien's Thai
21 Federal
White Rainbow

Reservations Not Accepted

Acapulco
Al Forno
Anchovies
Angel's
Anthony's Pier 4
Averof
Bangkok Bistro
Bangkok Cuisine
Barnacle
Bel Canto
Bertucci's Pizza
Black Dog Tavern
Blacksmith House
Blue Point Oyster Bar
Bluestone Bistro
Border Cafe
Boston Sail Loft
Botolph's on Tremont
Bull & Finch Pub
Cactus Club
Cafe China
Cafe Rouge
Caffe Lampara
Cambridge Sail Loft
Caserta's Pizza
Charlie's Sandwich
Chau Chow
Chili's
Circle Pizza
Commonwealth Brewing
Cornwall's
Daily Catch
Dali
East Coast Grill
Eastern Pier Seafood
Elsie's
Galeria Umberto
Gardner Museum Cafe
Giacomo's
Green Street Grill
Happy Haddock
Hard Rock Cafe
Jae's Cafe & Grill
Jimmy Mac's
La Espanola
La Groceria
Legal Sea Foods
Lucky's
Marshside
Mary Chung
Massimino's
Mexican Cuisine
Mr. Bartley's
Nadia's Eastern Star
Navona
Neighborhood Restaurant
New Bridge Cafe
Newport Grille
New Yorker Diner
Oasis Cafe
Olives
Pentimento
Piccolo Venezia
Pot Au Feu
Rubin's
Rudy's Cafe
Sabra
Salty Dog
Sami's 24 Hrs.
S&S Restaurant
Spaghetti Club, The

Star of Siam
Tandoor House
TGI Friday's
Thai Cuisine
Troyka
224 Boston St.
Villa Francesca
Village Fish
Village Smokehouse
Willow Pond Kitchen
Zuma Tex-Mex Cafe

Romantic Spots

Another Season
Aujourd'hui
Bay Tower Room
Black Dog Tavern
Blue Strawbery
Buteco
Cafe Budapest
Casa Mexico
Casa Romero
Chanticleer
Charles Restaurant
Chez Jean
Chez Nous
Chillingsworth
Colorado Public Library
Cornucopia
Cottonwood Cafe
Cranberry Moose
Dali
Davide
Davio's
Dom's
Du Barry
Felicia's
Genji
G'vanni's
Hampshire House
High Brewster
Hungry I
Icarus
Jasper's
Julien
Le Bellecoeur
Le Petit Auberge
L'Etoile
Locke-Ober Cafe
L'Osteria
Lucia's Ristorante
Maison Robert
Mamma Maria
Michela's
Mill Falls
Mister Leung's
Navona
Palmer's
Parker's
Plaza Dining Room
Rarities
Ristorante Toscano
Ritz Dining Room
Rosalie's
Rowes Wharf
Seasons
Second Story
Sfuzzi
Sherborn Inn
Siam Cuisine
Sol Azteca
St. Botolph
Top of the Hub
29 Newbury
21 Federal
Villa Francesca
White Rainbow

Saturday Dining
(B = brunch,
L = lunch)

Acapulco (L)
Acropolis (L)
Ahan-Thai (L)
Aku Aku (L)
Alexander's (L)
Amarin II (L)
Anthony's Pier 4 (L)

Ararat (L)
Atlantic Fish Co. (B,L)
Averof (B)
Azita (L)
B&D Deli (B,L)
Bangkok Cuisine (L)
Barbeques Int'l (L)
Barnacle (L)
Bel Canto (L)
Bennett Street Cafe (L)
Bennigan's (L)
Bernard's (L)
Bertucci's Pizza (L)
Black Dog Tavern (B,L)
Black Pearl (L)
Black Rose (L)
Blacksmith House (B,L)
Blue Diner (L)
Blue Wave (L)
Bob the Chef (L)
Boodle's of Boston (L)
Border Cafe (L)
Boston Sail Loft (L)
Botolph's (L)
Brandy Pete's (L)
Bridge Street Cafe (L)
Bristol Lounge (L)
Brodie's Cafe (L)
Buster's Barbecue (L)
Cactus Club (B,L)
Cafe Escadrille (L)
Cafe Fleuri (L)
Cafe Florian (L)
Cafe Paradiso (L)
Cafe Promenade (L)
Cafe Rose (L)
Cafe Rouge (L)
Cafe Suisse (L)
Caffe Lampara (L)
Caffe Luna (L)
Caffe Vittoria (L)
Callahan's (L)
Cambridge Sail Loft (L)
Cantin Abruzzi (L)
Cao Palace (L)

Capucino's (L)
Casa Mexico (L)
Caserta's Pizza (L)
Changsho (L)
Charley's Saloon (L)
Charlie's Sandwich (L)
Chatterley's (L)
Chau Chow (L)
Chef Chang's House (L)
Chef Chow's House (L)
Cherrystones (B,L)
Chili's (L)
Chillingsworth (L)
China Gate (L)
Ciaobella (L)
Circle Pizza (L)
Cityside (L)
Clarke Cooke House (L)
Clarke's (B)
Commonwealth Brew. (L)
Copley's (L)
Cornwall's (L)
Cottonwood Cafe (L)
Cranberry Moose (L)
Cricket's (B,L)
Davio's (L)
Division Sixteen (L)
Donatello's (L)
Du Barry (L)
Durgin Park (L)
Eagle Brook (L)
Eastern Pier (L)
Elsie's (L)
Ethiopian Rest. (L)
European Rest. (L)
57 Restaurant (L)
Five North Square (L)
Five Seasons (L)
Florence's Rest. (L)
Four Seas (L)
Freestones (L)
Frogg Lane (L)
Fuddrucker's (B,L)
Galeria Umberto (L)
Galley Rest. (L)

Genji (L)
Giannino's (L)
Gill's Grill (L)
Goemon (L)
Golden Palace (L)
Golden Temple (L)
Gourmeli's (L)
Grape Vine (L)
Great Stuff (B,L)
Grendel's Den (L)
Grill 23 (L)
G'vanni's (L)
Gyosai (L)
Gyuhama (L)
Hampshire House (L)
Hanmiok (L)
Happy Haddock (L)
Hard Rock Cafe (L)
Harvard Gardens (L)
Harvest (L)
Hemenway's (L)
Hilltop Steak House (L)
Houlihan's (L)
House of Siam (L)
Il Dolce Momento (L)
Imperial Tea Hse. (B,L)
India Pavilion (L)
India Royal (L)
Iruna (L)
Jacob Wirth (L)
Jae's Cafe (L)
J.C. Hillary's (L)
Jimbo's Fish Shanty (L)
Jimmy Mac's (L)
Jimmy's Harborside (L)
Joe's American (B,L)
Johnny D's (L)
Jonah's (L)
Joseph's Aquarium (L)
Joyce Chen (L)
Julien (L)
Kabuki (L)
Kebab-N-Kurry (L)

Ken's Steak House (L)
Kowloon (B,L)
La Espanola (B,L)
La Groceria (L)
Landing, The (L)
Las Brisas (L)
Last Hurrah (L)
La Trattoria (L)
Legal Sea Foods (L)
Le Grand Cafe (B,L)
Le Petit Auberge (L)
Loading Zone (L)
Los Andes (L)
Lucia's Ristorante (L)
Lucky Garden (L)
Lyceum Bar & Grill (L)
Magic Pan (L)
Mamma Maria (L)
Marshside (B,L)
Mary Chung (L)
Masada (L)
Massimino's (L)
Mateo's (L)
Mattapoisett Inn (L)
Mexican Cuisine (L)
Ming Garden (L)
Miyako (L)
Modern Diner (L)
Moon Villa (L)
Mr. Bartley's (L)
Museum Restaurant (L)
Neighborhood Rest. (L)
New Bridge Cafe (L)
Newbury Steak House (L)
New House of Toy (L)
New Korea (L)
Newport Grille (L)
Newtowne Grille (L)
New Yorker Diner (L)
Nicole (L)
Noble House (L)
No Name (L)
Oasis Cafe (B,L)

O'Fado (L)	Skipjack's (L)
Oh Calcutta (L)	Soom Thai (L)
On the Park (B)	Sorrento's (L)
Open Sesame (L)	Spaghetti Club (L)
Ottavio's (B)	Sports Depot (L)
Pagliuca's (L)	Stage Deli (L)
Paparazzi (B,L)	Stars Ocean (L)
Parker's (L)	St. Botolph (L)
Pattaya (L)	St. Cloud (L)
Peking Garden (L)	Stockyard, The (L)
Pentimento (B)	Streets Cafe (L)
Pho Pasteur (L)	Sultan's Kitchen (L)
Piccolo Venezia (L)	Sunset Cafe (L)
Porterhouse Cafe (L)	Sunset Grill (L)
Portugalia (B,L)	Sushi-Nagoya (L)
Pour House (L)	Ta Chien (L)
Rama Thai (L)	Taiwan Taste
Rebecca's (L)	Takeshima (L)
Red Lion (L)	Tam O'Shanter (L)
Ristorante Toscano (L)	Tandoor House (L)
Ritz Cafe (L)	Tapas (L)
Ritz Dining Room (L)	Taste of India (L)
Rocco's (L)	Ten Huntington (L)
Roka (L)	TGI Friday's (B,L)
Rowes Wharf (L)	Thai Cuisine (L)
Rudy's Cafe (L)	Thai House (L)
Sabra (L)	Thornton's (B,L)
Sakura-bana (L)	Tien's Thai (L)
Salty Dog (L)	Tim's Tavern (L)
Sami's 24 Hrs. (L)	Top of the Hub (L)
S&S Rest. (B,L)	Topper's (B)
Saraceno's (L)	Toscano's (L)
Sawasdee (L)	Troyka (L)
Sculler's Grille (L)	Turner Fisheries (L)
Seaside Rest. (L)	29 Newbury (L)
Serendipity III (L)	21 Federal (L)
Sevens, The (L)	Union Grill (L)
Sfuzzi (L)	Union Oyster House (L)
Sherborn Inn (L)	Union Street Cafe (L)
Shilla (L)	Venus Seafood (B,L)
Siam Cuisine (L)	Verona (L)
Sibel (B)	Via Veneto (L)
Skewers, The (L)	Victoria Diner (B,L)

Victoria Station (L)
Viet Restaurant (L)
Village Fish, The (L)
Village Smokehouse (L)
Vin & Eddie's (L)
Vinny Marino's (L)
Warren Tavern (L)
Washington Street Bar (L)
Weylu's (L)
White Horse Tavern (L)
Willow Pond Kitchen (L)
Winery Restaurant (L)
Wursthaus, The (B,L)
Yangtze River (L)
Yelena (L)
Yenching Palace (L)
Zuma Tex-Mex Cafe (L)

Senior Appeal

Alexander's
Anthony's Pier 4
B&D Deli
Barrett's
Bennett Street Cafe
Bernard's
Boylston's
Bristol Lounge
Cafe Paradiso
Cafe Promenade
Cafe Rouge
Cafe Suisse
Capucino's
Charles Restaurant
Chef Chang's House
Chef Chow's House
Chillingsworth
Ciro's
Copley's
Cranberry Moose
Da Natale
Dover Sea Grille
D.R. Brown's
European Restaurant
57 Restaurant
Florence's Restaurant
Galley Restaurant
Gardner Museum Cafe
Goemon
Golden Temple
Great Stuff
Happy Haddock
High Brewster
Jimmy's Harborside
Joe Tecce's
Ken's Steak House
Kowloon
La Summa
Legal Sea Foods
Magic Pan
Marshside
Mass Bay Company
Mill Falls
Ming Garden
Museum Restaurant
Noble House
No Name
O'Fado
On the Square
Parker's
P.A. Seafood
Pattaya
Peacock Restaurant
Peking Garden
Pillar House
Rama Thai
Regatta of Cotuit
Regatta of Falmouth
Ritz Cafe
Ritz Dining Room
Rowes Wharf
Rubin's
Sabra
S&S Restaurant
Saraceno's
Sawasdee

Sherborn Inn
Skipjack's
Spinnaker Italia
Stage Deli
Ta Chien
Takeshima
Venetian Garden
Venus Seafood
Verona
Villa Francesca
Village Fish, The
Vin & Eddie's
Weylu's
Yangtze River

Sidewalk Cafes

Acapulco
Alexander's
Blue Point Oyster Bar
Bnu
Cactus Club
Cafe Florian
Clarke Cooke House
Davio's
Goemon
Harvard Bookstore Cafe
Jacob Wirth Restaurant
Jae's Cafe & Grill
Legal Sea Foods
Michela's
Mill Falls
Serendipity III
Sibel
Sorrento's
Thornton's
29 Newbury
Victoria Station

Sleepers
(Good to excellent food, but little known)

Giacomo's
Icarus
Jae's Cafe
On the Square
Rama Thai
Rowes Wharf
224 Boston St.
Venus Seafood

Smoking Prohibited

Ahan-Thai
Atlantic Fish Co.
Bernardo's
Blacksmith House
Cafe Budapest
Cherrystones
Chez Nous
Daily Catch
Ethiopian Restaurant
Gardner Museum Cafe
Hampshire House
Il Capriccio
India Pavilion
Jonah's
Little Osaka
Lucky Garden
Medieval Manor
New Korea
Olives
On the Park
Pentimento
Pillar House
Pot Au Feu
Shogun
Sultan's Kitchen
Village Fish, The

Sunday Dining

(B = brunch;
L = lunch;
D = dinner; in addition to hotels and most chains)

Acapulco (L,D)
Acropolis (L,D)
Ahan-Thai (L,D)
Aku Aku (L,D)
Alexander's (D)
Amarin II (D)
Anchovies (B,L)
Anthony's (L,D)
Arrows (D)
Atlantic Fish Co. (B,L,D)
Aujourd'hui (B,D)
B&D Deli (B,L,D)
Bangkok Bistro (D)
Bangkok Cuisine (L,D)
Barbeques Int'l (D)
Barnacle (L,D)
Barrett's (B,D)
Bel Canto (L,D)
Bella Napoli (D)
Bello Mondo (B)
Bennett Street Cafe (B,L,D)
Bennigan's (B,L,D)
Bernardo's (D)
Bernard's (B,D)
Bertucci's Pizza (L,D)
Biba (B,L,D)
Bishop's (D)
Black Dog Tavern (B,D)
Black Forest Cafe (B)
Black Pearl (L,D)
Black Rose (B,L,D)
Blue Diner (B)
Bluestone Bistro (D)
Blue Strawbery (D)
Blue Wave (B,L,D)
Bnu (D)
Bob the Chef (L,D)
Boodle's (L,D)
Border Cafe (L,D)
Boston Sail Loft (B)
Brandy Pete's (B,L,D)
Bridge Street Cafe (B,D)
Bristol Lounge (B,D)
Brodie's Cafe (L,D)
Buoniconti's (D)
Buster's Barbecue (L,D)
Buteco (D)
Cactus Club (B,L,D)
Cafe Amalfi (D)
Cafe Budapest (D)
Cafe China (D)
Cafe Fleuri (B,D)
Cafe Florian (B,L,D)
Cafe Paradiso (D)
Cafe Promenade (B,D)
Cafe Rose (L,D)
Cafe Rouge (B,L)
Cafe Suisse (L)
Caffe Lampara (L,D)
Caffe Luna (B,L,D)
Caffe Vittoria (L,D)
Callahan's (L,D)
Cambridge Sail Loft (B)
Cantin Abruzzi (D)
Cantina Italiana (D)
Cape Neddick Inn (B,D)
Capucino's (B,L,D)
Carlo Marino's (D)
Casa Mexico (D)
Casa Portugal (D)
Casa Romero (D)
Caserta's Pizza (L,D)
Changsho (L,D)
Chanticleer (B)
Charles Rest. (D)
Charley's (B,L,D)
Chart House (D)
Chatterley's (L,D)
Chau Chow (L,D)
Chef Chang's (L,D)

Chef Chow's (L,D)	Four Seas (L,D)
Cherrystones (B,L,D)	Freestones (L,D)
Chili's (L,D)	Frogg Lane (L,D)
Chillingsworth (B,L,D)	Fuddrucker's (B,L,D)
China Gate (L,D)	Galley Rest. (L,D)
Ciaobella (B,D)	Gardner Museum (L)
Circle Pizza (L,D)	Genji (L,D)
Ciro & Sal's (D)	Giacomo's (D)
Ciro's (D)	Giannino's (L,D)
Cityside (B,L,D)	Gill's Grill (B,D)
Claddagh (B)	Golden Palace (L)
Clarke Cooke (B,L,D)	Golden Temple (L,D)
Clarke's (B)	Gourmeli's (L)
Club Cafe (B,L,D)	Great Stuff (B,L,D)
Colorado Pub. Lib. (D)	Grendel's Den (B,L,D)
Commonwealth (L,D)	Grill 23 (D)
Coolidge Cnr. Club. (B)	G'vanni's (L,D)
Copley's (B,D)	Gyosai (L,D)
Cornwall's (B)	Gyuhama (L,D)
Cottonwood Cafe (B,L,D)	Hampshire House (B,D)
Cranberry Moose (B,D)	Happy Haddock (L,D)
Cricket's (B,L,D)	Hard Rock Cafe (L,D)
Dali (D)	Harvard Bkst. (B,L,D)
D'Artagnan (L,D)	Harvard Gardens (L)
Davide (D)	Harvest (B,D)
Davio's (L,D)	Hemenway's (D)
Division Sixteen (B,D)	High Brewster (B)
Domenico's (D)	Hilltop Steak Hse. (L,D)
Dom's (D)	Houlihan's (L,D)
Donatello's (D)	Ho Yuen Ting (D)
Dover Sea Grille (D)	House of Siam (D)
Du Barry (D)	Hungry I (B,D)
Durgin Park (L,D)	Icarus (B,D)
Eagle Brook (L,D)	Il Capriccio (D)
Eastern Pier (L,D)	Il Dolce Momento (L,D)
Elsie's (L)	Imperial Tea Hse. (L,D)
Ethiopian Rest. (L,D)	India Pavilion (D)
European Rest. (L,D)	India Royal (L,D)
Felicia's (L,D)	Jacob Wirth (B,L,D)
57 Rest. (D)	Jae's Cafe (B,D)
Five North Sq. (L,D)	J.C. Hillary's (B,D)
Five Seasons (B,D)	Jimbo's Fish (L,D)
Florence's (L)	Jimmy Mac's (B,D)

Jimmy's Harbor. (L,D)
Joe's American (B,L,D)
Joe Tecce's (D)
Johnny D's (B)
Jonah's (B,L,D)
Joseph's Aquarium (L,D)
Joyce Chen (L,D)
Kabuki (D)
Kebab-N-Kurry (D)
Ken's Steak House (D)
King & I (D)
Kowloon (B,L)
Kyoto (D)
La Espanola (B,L,D)
La Groceria (D)
Landing, The (B,D)
La Rivage (B,D)
Las Brisas (B,D)
La Trattoria (B,D)
Le Bellecoeur (B)
Legal Sea Foods (L,D)
Le Grand Cafe (B,L,D)
Le Grenier (B,L)
Le Petit Auberge (B,D)
L'Etoile (B,D)
Loading Zone (B,L,D)
Locke-Ober Cafe (D)
Los Andes (L,D)
Lucia's Rist. (L,D)
Lucky Garden (L,D)
Lyceum Bar (B,D)
Magic Pan (B,L,D)
Mamma Maria (D)
Marshside (B,L)
Mary Chung (L,D)
Masada (L,D)
Mass Bay Co. (D)
Mateo's (D)
Matsu-ya (D)
Mattapoisett Inn (B,D)
Mexican Cuisine (D)
Michael's Waterfront (D)
Ming Garden (L,D)

Mister Leung's (D)
Miyako (D)
Modern Diner (L)
Montien (D)
Moon Villa (L,D)
Morton's (D)
Mother Anna's (D)
Mr. Bartley's (L,D)
Museum Restaurant (L)
Nadia's (D)
Navona (B,D)
Neighborhood Rest. (L,D)
New Bridge Cafe (L,D)
Newbury Stkhse. (L,D)
New House of Toy (L)
New Korea (L,D)
Newport Grille (B,D)
Newtowne Grille (L,D)
New Yorker Diner (B,L)
Noble House (L,D)
No Name (L,D)
Oasis Cafe (B)
O'Fado (L,D)
Oh Calcutta (D)
Olives (D)
On the Park (B,D)
On the Square (D)
Open Sesame (D)
Ottavio's (B)
Pagliuca's (L)
Paparazzi (B,L,D)
Parker's (B)
P.A. Seafood (D)
Pattaya (B,D)
Peking Garden (L,D)
Pentimento (B)
Pho Pasteur (L,D)
Piccolo Venezia (L,D)
Porterhouse Cafe (D)
Portugalia (B,L,D)
Pour House (B,D)
Promises To Keep (D)
Rama Thai (D)

Rebecca's (B,D)	Spinnaker Italia (B,D)
Red Lion (B,D)	Sports Depot (B,D)
Redbones (D)	Stage Deli (L,D)
Regatta/Cotuit (D)	Star of Siam (D)
Regatta/Falmouth (D)	Stars Ocean (L,D)
Ristorante Toscano (D)	St. Botolph (B,D)
Ritz Cafe (B,D)	St. Cloud (B,D)
Ritz Dining Room (B,D)	Stellina's (D)
Rocco's (L,D)	Straight Wharf (D)
Roka (D)	Streets Cafe (L,D)
Rosalie's (B,D)	Sunset Cafe (L,D)
Rowes Wharf (B,D)	Sunset Grill (B,D)
Rubin's (B,L,D)	Sushi-Nagoya (D)
Rudy's Cafe (L,D)	Ta Chien (L,D)
Sabra (L,D)	Takeshima (D)
Sakura-bana (D)	Taiwan Taste (L,D)
Sally Ling's (D)	Tam O'Shanter (B,D)
Salty Dog (B,D)	Tandoor House (L,D)
Sami's 24 Hrs. (L,D)	Tapas (B,D)
S&S Rest. (B,L,D)	Taste of India (L,D)
Saporito (D)	Tatsukichi (D)
Saraceno's (L,D)	TGI Friday's (B,L,D)
Sawasdee (D)	Thai Cuisine (D)
Sculler's Grille (B,D)	Thai House (L,D)
Seaside (B,D)	Thornton's (B,L,D)
Seasons (D)	Tien's Thai (D)
Second Story (B)	Top of the Hub (B,D)
Seoul House (D)	Troyka (L,D)
Serendipity III (B,D)	Turner Fisheries (B,D)
Sevens, The (L,D)	29 Newbury (B,D)
Sfuzzi (B,D)	21 Federal (L,D)
Shalimar (B,D)	224 Boston St. (B)
Sherborn Inn (L,D)	Union Grill (B,D)
Shilla (L,D)	Union Oyster (B,D)
Shogun (D)	Union St. Cafe (B,D)
Siam Cuisine (D)	Upstairs/Pudding (B)
Sibel (B,D)	Venetian Garden (D)
Skewers, The (L,D)	Venus Seafood (B,L,D)
Skipjack's (B,L,D)	Verona (L,D)
Sol Azteca (D)	Veronique (B,L,D)
Soom Thai (D)	Via Veneto (L,D)
Sorrento's (L,D)	Victoria Diner (B,L,D)
Spaghetti Club (L,D)	Victoria Station (B,D)

Viet Restaurant (L,D)
Villa Francesca (D)
Village Fish (D)
Village Smokehse. (D)
Vin & Eddie's (L,D)
Vinny Marino's (B,L,D)
Warren Tavern (L,D)
Washington St. Bar (B,D)
Weylu's (L,D)
White Barn Inn (D)
White Horse (B,D)
Willow Pond (L,D)
Winery (L,D)
Wursthaus (B,L,D)
Yangtze River (L,D)
Yelena (L,D)
Yenching Palace (L,D)
Zuma Tex-Mex (L,D)

Takeout
(Almost all ethnics, BBQs, diners, burger joints and pizzerias sell takeout, as do the following)

Acropolis
Aku Aku
Alberta's Cafe
Amarin II
Averof
Back Bay Bistro
B&D Deli
Bangkok Bistro
Bangkok Cuisine
Barbeques Int'l
Bel Canto
Bertucci's Pizza
Blue Diner
Blue Wave
Bob the Chef
Bridge Street Cafe
Brodie's Cafe
Buster's Barbecue
Buteco
Cafe China
Cafe Florian
Caffe Lampara
Caffe Luna
Caffe Vittoria
Cajun Yankee
Cantina Italiana
Cao Palace
Capucino's
Carl's Pagoda
Casa Elena
Caserta's Pizza
Changsho
Charles Restaurant
Charley's Saloon
Chau Chow
Chef Chang's House
Chef Chow's House
Cherrystones
Chez Jean
China Gate
Circle Pizza
Cityside
Daily Catch
Davio's
Division Sixteen
Domenico's
Dom's
Donatello's
D.R. Brown's
East Coast Grill
Eastern Pier Seafood
European Restaurant
Five Seasons
Four Seas
Freestones
Galeria Umberto
Giacomo's
Gill's Grill
Goemon
Grape Vine
Great Stuff

- Green Street Grill
- G'vanni's
- Gyuhama
- Hanmiok
- Happy Haddock
- Harvard Bookstore Cafe
- Harvest
- Ho Yuen Ting
- Imperial Tea House
- India Pavilion
- India Royal
- Jae's Cafe & Grill
- Jimbo's Fish Shanty
- Jimmy Mac's
- Joe's American Bar
- Joe Tecce's
- Karoun
- Kebab-N-Kurry
- La Espanola
- La Trattoria
- Le Bellecoeur
- Legal Sea Foods
- Le Grand Cafe
- L'Osteria
- Lucia's Ristorante
- Masada
- Massimino's
- Mateo's
- Mexican Cuisine
- Michael's Waterfront
- Milk Street Cafe
- Miyako
- Modern Diner
- Mother Anna's
- Mr. Bartley's
- Nadia's Eastern Star
- Neighborhood Restaurant
- New Bridge Cafe
- Newtowne Grille
- New Yorker Diner
- No Name
- Oasis Cafe
- O'Fado
- Open Sesame
- P.A. Seafood
- Peacock Restaurant
- Pentimento
- Porterhouse Cafe
- Portugalia
- Pour House
- Pushcart
- Rebecca's
- Red Lion
- Redbones
- Roka
- Rubin's
- Rudy's Cafe
- Sabra
- Salty Dog
- Sami's 24 Hrs.
- S&S Restaurant
- Seaside Restaurant
- Serendipity III
- Shalimar of India
- Sibel
- Skewers, The
- Skipjack's
- Sol Azteca
- Stage Deli
- St. Botolph
- St. Cloud
- Stellina's
- Streets Cafe
- Sultan's Kitchen
- Sunset Cafe
- Sunset Grill & Tap
- Tam O'Shanter, The
- TGI Friday's
- Thornton's
- Tim's Tavern
- Top of the Hub
- Troyka
- 29 Newbury
- 21 Federal
- 224 Boston St.
- Union Grill

Union Oyster House
Union Street Cafe
Venus Seafood
Verona
Victoria Diner
Village Fish, The
Village Smokehouse
Washington Street Bar
Willow Pond Kitchen
Zuma Tex-Mex Cafe

Teas

Blacksmith House
Bristol Lounge
Cafe Florian
Cafe Promenade
Cafe Rouge
Cafe Suisse
Clarke Cooke House
Harvard Bookstore Cafe
Ritz Dining Room

Teenagers & Other Youthful Spirits

Bangkok Bistro
Bel Canto
Bennigan's
Bertucci's Pizza
Black Forest Cafe
Bluestone Bistro
Border Cafe
Boston Sail Loft
Cafe De Paris
Cafe Paradiso
Cantin Abruzzi
Chef Chow's House
Chili's
Coolidge Cnr. Club.
Copley's
Cricket's
Dad's Beantown Diner
Dynasty
European Restaurant
Fajita Rita's
Fuddrucker's
Galeria Umberto
Golden Temple
Great Stuff
Grendel's Den
Hard Rock Cafe
Houlihan's
Joyce Chen
Karoun
Lucky Garden
Marshside
Medieval Manor
Moon Villa
Mr. Bartley's
New Bridge Cafe
New Yorker Diner
No Name
Peking Garden
Porterhouse Cafe
Redbones
Rubin's
Sabra
Salty Dog
S&S Restaurant
Santarpio's Pizza
Serendipity III
Skewers, The
Spaghetti Club, The
Sports Depot, The
Stage Deli
Steak/Neighborhood
Ta Chien
Takeshima
TGI Friday's
Thornton's
Tim's Tavern
Venus Seafood
Victoria Station
Village Fish, The
Village Smokehouse
Weylu's

Visitors on Expense Accounts

Anthony's Pier 4
Aujourd'hui
Biba
Cafe Budapest
Chanticleer
Chillingsworth
Grill 23
Gyosai
Jasper's
Julien
L'Espalier
L'Etoile
Locke-Ober Cafe
Maison Robert
Michela's
Morton's of Chicago
Parker's
Plaza Dining Room
Ports
Rarities
Ritz Dining Room
Sakura-bana
Seasons
Tatsukichi
21 Federal
Upstairs/Pudding

Wheelchair Access
(Check for bathroom access; almost all hotels, plus the following)

Ahan-Thai
Aku Aku
Amarin II
Anchovies
Anthony's Pier 4
Atlantic Fish Co.
Aujourd'hui
Averof
Back Bay Bistro
B&D Deli
Barrett's
Bay Tower Room
Bel Canto
Bello Mondo
Bennett Street Cafe
Bennigan's
Bernard's
Bernardo's
Bertucci's Pizza
Biba
Bisuteki
Black Forest Cafe
Black Goose
Black Pearl
Black Rose
Blue Wave
Bnu
Boodle's of Boston
Border Cafe
Botolph's on Tremont
Boylston's
Brandy Pete's
Bridge Street Cafe
Bristol Lounge
Brodie's Cafe
Buoniconti's
Buster's Barbecue
Buteco
Cactus Club
Cafe Brazil
Cafe Budapest
Cafe De Paris
Cafe Fleuri
Cafe Promenade
Cafe Rose
Cafe Rouge
Cafe Suisse
Caffe Lampara
Caffe Luna
Caffe Vittoria
Callahan's
Candleworks

Cantina Italiana
Cao Palace
Cape Neddick Inn
Capucino's
Carlo Marino's
Casa Elena
Casa Portugal
Changsho
Charles Restaurant
Charley's Saloon
Chart House
Chatterley's
Chef Chang's House
Chef Chow's House
Cherrystones
Chez Jean
Chez Nous
Chili's
Ciro's
Cityside
Claddagh
Clarke's
Club Cafe
Colorado Public Library
Commonwealth Brewing
Copley's
Cornucopia
Cornwall's
Cottonwood Cafe
Cranberry Moose
Cricket's
Dakota's
Dali
Da Natale
Davide
Davio's
Division Sixteen
Domenico's
Donatello's
Dover Sea Grille
D.R. Brown's
Eagle Brook Saloon
East Coast Grill

Eastern Pier Seafood
Ethiopian Restaurant
European Restaurant
Fajita Rita's
Felicia's
57 Restaurant
Finally Michael's
Five North Square
Florence's Restaurant
Freestones
Frogg Lane
Fuddrucker's
Gardner Museum Cafe
Genji
Giannino's
Goemon
Golden Temple
Grape Vine
Great Stuff
G'vanni's
Gyosai
Hamersley's Bistro
Hampshire House
Hanmiok
Happy Haddock
Hard Rock Cafe
Harvard Bookstore Cafe
Harvard Gardens
Harvard Street Grill
Harvest
Hemenway's
High Brewster
Hilltop Steak House
Houlihan's
House of Siam
Il Capriccio
Il Dolce Momento
Il Giardino Cafe
India Royal
Jacob Wirth Restaurant
Jae's Cafe & Grill
Jasper's
J.C. Hillary's Ltd.

Joe Tecce's	Olives
Jonah's	On the Square
Joseph's Aquarium	Open Sesame
Joyce Chen	Ottavio's
Kabuki	Pagliuca's Restaurant
Karoun	Palmer's
King & Kowloon	Parker's
La Groceria	P.A. Seafood
Landing, The	Pattaya
Las Brisas	Peking Garden
Last Hurrah	Pho Pasteur
La Trattoria	Plaza Dining Room
Le Bellecoeur	Ponte Vecchio
Le Bocage	Porterhouse Cafe
Legal Sea Foods	Ports
Little Osaka	Portugalia
Loading Zone	Pour House
Locke-Ober Cafe	Promises To Keep
Los Andes	Rama Thai
L'Osteria	Rarities
Lyceum Bar & Grill	Red Lion
Marshside	Redbones
Masada	Regatta of Falmouth
Mass Bay Company	Rita's Place
Massimino's	Ritz Cafe
Medieval Manor	Ritz Dining Room
Michela's	Rocco's
Mill Falls	Roka
Ming Garden	Rosalie's
Mister Leung's	Rowes Wharf
Modern Diner	Rubin's
Morton's of Chicago	Rudy's Cafe
Museum Restaurant	Sablone's Veal 'n Vintage
Nara Restaurant	Sabra
Navona	Sally Ling's
New Bridge Cafe	Sami's 24 Hrs.
New House of Toy	S&S Restaurant
New Korea	Santarpio's Pizza
Nicole	Saporito
Noble House	Saraceno's
No Name	Sawasdee
Oasis Cafe	Schroeder's
O'Fado	Sculler's Grille

Seaside Restaurant
Seasons
Serendipity III
Sfuzzi
Shalimar of India
Sherborn Inn
Sibel
Skipjack's
Soom Thai
Sorrento's
Spaghetti Club, The
Spinnaker Italia
Sports Depot, The
Stage Deli
Stars Ocean
St. Cloud
Steak/Neighborhood
Stellina's
Stockyard, The
Straight Wharf
Sultan's Kitchen
Ta Chien
Takeshima
Tapas
Taste of India
Ten Huntington
Thai House
Thornton's
Tien's Thai
Top of the Hub
Toscano's
Turner Fisheries
21 Federal
Upstairs/Pudding
Venus Seafood
Via Veneto
Village Fish, The
Village Smokehouse
Vin & Eddie's
Vinny Marino's
Washington Street Bar
Weylu's
White Rainbow
Willow Pond Kitchen
Wursthaus, The
Yangtze River
Yelena
Yenching Palace
Zuma Tex-Mex Cafe

Winning Wine Lists

Al Forno
Anthony's Pier 4
Aujourd'hui
Back Bay Bistro
Biba
Black Pearl
Blue Point Oyster Bar
Cafe Escadrille
Cafe Fleuri
Chanticleer
Chillingsworth
Colorado Public Library
Cornucopia
Dali
Finally Michael's
Grill 23
Hamersley's Bistro
Harvest
Icarus
Jasper's
Jimmy's Harborside
Julien
Le Bocage
Legal Seafood
L'Etoile
Locke-Ober Cafe
Lucia's Ristorante
Lucky's
Maison Robert
Mamma Maria
Michael's Waterfront
Michela's
Mill Falls
Olives

On the Square
Parker's
Pillar House
Plaza Dining Room
Pot Au Feu
Rarities
Ristorante Toscano
Ritz Cafe
Ritz Dining Room
Rocco's
Rowes Wharf
Seasons
798 Main
Skipjack's
St. Botolph
St. Cloud
Upstairs/Pudding
Via Veneto

Worth a Trip

MAINE
Cape Neddick
  Cape Neddick Inn
Kennebunkport
  White Barn Inn
Portland
  Alberta's Cafe
Ogunquit
  Arrows
MASSACHUSETTS
Abington
  Vin & Eddie's
Cape Cod
  Chillingsworth
  Cranberry Moose
  High Brewster
  Regatta of Cotuit
  Regatta of Falmouth
Gloucester
  White Rainbow
Marblehead
  Barnacle

Martha's Vineyard
  Black Dog Tavern
  L'Etoile
Nantucket
  Chanticleer
  Straight Wharf
  Topper's
  21 Federal
Sherborn
  Sherborn Inn
South Dartmouth
  Bridge Street Cafe
NEW HAMPSHIRE
Portsmouth
  Strawbery Court
RHODE ISLAND
Newport
  Clarke Cooke House
Providence
  Al Forno
  Angel's
  Blue Point Oyster Bar
  Lucky's

Young Children
(Besides the normal fast-food places)

B&D Deli
Bel Canto
Bennett Street Cafe
Bennigan's
Bernard's
Bertucci's Pizza
Bishop's
Bluestone Bistro
Border Cafe
Boston Sail Loft
Buteco
Cafe De Paris
Cafe Paradiso
Caffe Vittoria
Capucino's
Changsho

- Chili's
- Circle Pizza
- Coolidge Cnr. Club.
- Da Natale
- Demo's Restaurant
- Durgin Park
- European Restaurant
- Fajita Rita's
- Four Seas
- Fuddrucker's
- Galeria Umberto
- Galley Restaurant
- Goemon
- Golden Temple
- Great Stuff
- Happy Haddock
- Hard Rock Cafe
- Hilltop Steak House
- Houlihan's
- Imperial Tea House
- Jimbo's Fish Shanty
- Joyce Chen
- Karoun
- Kowloon
- Kyoto Steak House
- La Espanola
- Las Brisas
- Legal Sea Foods
- Loading Zone
- L'Osteria
- Marshside
- Ming Garden
- Mr. Bartley's
- Neighborhood Restaurant
- Noble House
- No Name
- Oasis Cafe
- O'Fado
- Pattaya
- Peking Garden
- Pentimento
- Piccolo Venezia
- Porterhouse Cafe
- Portugalia
- Redbones
- Rubin's
- S&S Restaurant
- Santarpio's Pizza
- Sawasdee
- Serendipity III
- Shogun
- Siam Cuisine
- Skewers, The
- Skipjack's
- Sol Azteca
- Sorrento's
- Sports Depot, The
- Stage Deli
- Stars Ocean
- Steak/Neighborhood
- Ta Chien
- Takeshima
- TGI Friday's
- Top of the Hub
- Union Oyster House
- Venus Seafood
- Verona
- Via Veneto
- Victoria Diner
- Victoria Station
- Villa Francesca
- Village Fish, The
- Village Smokehouse
- Vinny Marino's
- Washington Street Bar
- Weylu's
- Yangtze River

RATING SHEETS

To aid in your participation in our next *Survey*

| F | D | S | C |

| | | | $ |

Restaurant Name _____
Phone _____
Comments _____
_____
_____

| | | | $ |

Restaurant Name _____
Phone _____
Comments _____
_____
_____

| | | | $ |

Restaurant Name _____
Phone _____
Comments _____
_____
_____

| | | | $ |

Restaurant Name _____
Phone _____
Comments _____
_____
_____

| | | | $ |

Restaurant Name _____
Phone _____
Comments _____
_____
_____

| | | | $ |

Restaurant Name _____
Phone _____
Comments _____
_____
_____

			F	**D**	**S**	**C**

|_|_|_|$|

Restaurant Name _____
Phone _____
Comments _____
_____
_____

|_|_|_|$|

Restaurant Name _____
Phone _____
Comments _____
_____
_____

|_|_|_|$|

Restaurant Name _____
Phone _____
Comments _____
_____
_____

|_|_|_|$|

Restaurant Name _____
Phone _____
Comments _____
_____
_____

|_|_|_|$|

Restaurant Name _____
Phone _____
Comments _____
_____
_____

|_|_|_|$|

Restaurant Name _____
Phone _____
Comments _____
_____
_____

			F	**D**	**S**	**C**

			$

Restaurant Name _____
Phone _____
Comments _____
_____
_____

			$

Restaurant Name _____
Phone _____
Comments _____
_____
_____

			$

Restaurant Name _____
Phone _____
Comments _____
_____
_____

			$

Restaurant Name _____
Phone _____
Comments _____
_____
_____

			$

Restaurant Name _____
Phone _____
Comments _____
_____
_____

			$

Restaurant Name _____
Phone _____
Comments _____
_____
_____

WINE VINTAGE CHART 1979-1989

These ratings are designed to help you select wine to go with your meal. They are on the same 0 to 30 scale used throughout this Guide. The ratings reflect both the quality of the vintage year and the wine's readiness to drink. Thus, if a wine is not fully mature or is over the hill, its rating has been reduced. The ratings were prepared principally by our friend, Howard Strawitz, a law professor at the University of South Carolina.

WHITES	79	80	81	82	83	84	85	86	87	88	89
French:											
Burgundy	17	—	16	18	19	14	25	28	16	21	24
Loire Valley	—	—	—	—	—	—	19	18	15	20	23
Champagne	20	—	19	23	20	—	21	19	—	—	22
Sauternes	12	24	23	13	23	—	18	23	10	25	24
California:											
Chardonnay	—	16	14	13	13	22	24	27	24	26	24
REDS											
French:											
Bordeaux	22	13	25	27	24	15	25	24	21	21	21
Burgundy	18	20	16	20	25	14	27	16	21	20	19
Rhone	18	17	16	16	25	15	25	21	16	19	20
Beaujolais	—	—	—	—	—	—	21	22	23	24	26
California:											
Cabernet Sauvignon	20	23	21	23	18	26	25	23	24	18	19
Zinfandel	—	—	—	—	—	17	18	16	20	15	16
Italian:*											
Chianti	11	—	14	17	13	—	23	16	12	20	11
Piedmont	21	12	15	25	14	—	23	13	17	19	20

* Bargain sippers take note—Certain wines are reliable year in year out and are reasonably priced as well. These wines are best in the most recent vintages. They include: Alsacian Pinot Blancs, Cotes de Rhone, Muscadet, Bardolino, Valpolicella, Corvo, Spanish Rioja and California Zinfandel.